101 best campsites

for outdoor activities

alan rogers

Compiled by: Alan Rogers Guides Ltd

Designed by: Vine Design Ltd

© Alan Rogers Guides Ltd 2011

Published by: Alan Rogers Guides Ltd,
Spelmonden Old Oast, Goudhurst, Kent TN17 1HE

www.alanrogers.com
Tel: 01580 214000

British Library Cataloguing-in-Publication Data:
A catalogue record for this book is available from
the British Library.

ISBN 978-1-906215-60-6

Printed in Great Britain by
Stephens & George Print Group

contents

Introduction	4	Belgium	84
Spain	17	Netherlands	86
Portugal	23	Germany	93
Italy	25	Czech Republic	99
Slovenia	34	Slovakia	103
Hungary	39	Denmark	104
Austria	42	Norway	108
Switzerland	45	Sweden	113
France	50	Finland	116
United Kingdom	74	Index	124
Ireland	81		

Welcome to the Alan Rogers
'101' guides

The Alan Rogers guides have been helping campers and caravanners make informed decisions about their holiday destinations since 1968. Today, whether online or in print, Alan Rogers still provides an independent, impartial view, with detailed reports on each campsite.

With so much unfiltered, unqualified information freely available, the Alan Rogers perspective is invaluable to make sure you make the right choice for your holiday.

What is the '101' **series**?

At Alan Rogers, we know that readers have many and diverse interests, hobbies and particular requirements. And we know that our guides, featuring a total of some 3,000 campsites, can provide a bewildering choice from which it can be difficult to produce a shortlist of possible holiday destinations.

The Alan Rogers 101 guides are devised as a means of presenting a realistic, digestible number of great campsites, featured because of their suitability to a given theme.

This book remains first and foremost an authoritative guide to excellent campsites which offer great opportunities to enjoy a range of exciting outdoor activities.

101 **Best campsites for outdoor activities**

Campsites are all about being in the open air, enjoying wonderful natural surroundings. And, of course, time spent on a campsite lends itself to outdoor activities of all sorts, from 'conventional' sports like tennis, to activities often more associated with a holiday, such as kayaking or rafting, through to outward bound pursuits like orienteering and more specialist activities like sand yachting.

Recognising this, campsites have evolved hugely in recent years, investing in new sporting facilities, developing new services and attracting new activity-minded holiday makers.

This is partly due to leisure trends, partly to the influence of organisations like Center Parcs and the Duke of Edinburgh scheme and partly to commercial needs. Many campers are first and foremost activity enthusiasts, for whom staying on a campsite is simply a convenient means of enjoying their chosen activity. Others are 'die-hard' campers who also happen to enjoy a chosen activity.

Alan Rogers – in search
of 'the best'

Alan Rogers himself started off with the very specific aim of providing people with the necessary information to allow them to make an informed decision about their holiday destination. Today we still do that with a range of guides that now covers Europe's best campsites in 27 countries.

We work with campsites all day, every day. We visit campsites for inspection purposes (or even just for pleasure!). We know campsites 'inside out'.

We know which campsites would suit active families; which are great for get-away-from-it-all couples; we know which campsites are planning super new pool complexes; which campsites offer a fantastic menu in their on-site restaurant; which campsites allow you to launch a small boat from their slipway; which campsites have a decent playing area for kicking a ball around; which campsites have flat, grassy pitches and which have solid hard standings.

We also know which are good for fishing, golf, spas, children, nature and outdoor activities; which are close to the beach; and which welcome dogs. These particular themes form our '101' series.

All Alan Rogers guides (and our website) are respected for their independent, impartial and honest assessment. The reviews are prose-based, without overuse of indecipherable icons and symbols. Our simple aim is to help guide you to a campsite that matches best your requirements – often quite difficult in today's age of information overload.

What is the **best**?

The criteria we use when inspecting and selecting sites are numerous, but the most important by far is the question of good quality. People want different things from their choice of campsite, so campsite 'styles' vary dramatically: from small peaceful campsites in the heart of the countryside, to 'all singing, all dancing' sites in popular seaside resorts.

The size of the site, whether it's part of a chain or privately owned, makes no difference in terms of it being required to meet our exacting standards in respect of its quality and it being 'fit for purpose'. In other words, irrespective of the size of the site, or the number of facilities it offers, we consider and evaluate the welcome, the pitches, the sanitary facilities, the cleanliness, the general maintenance and even the location.

Expert opinions

We rely on our dedicated team of Site Assessors, all of whom are experienced campers, caravanners or motorcaravanners, to visit and recommend campsites. Each year they travel around Europe inspecting new campsites for Alan Rogers and re-inspecting the existing ones.

When planning
your **holiday...**

A holiday should always be a relaxing affair, and a campsite-based holiday particularly so. Our aim is for you to find the ideal campsite for your holiday, one that suits your requirements. All Alan Rogers guides provide a wealth of information, including some details supplied by campsite owners themselves, and the following points may help ensure that you plan a successful holiday.

Find out more

An Alan Rogers reference number (e.g. **FR12345**) is given for each campsite and can be useful for finding more information and pictures online at **www.alanrogers.com**
Simply enter this number in the 'Campsite Search' field on the Home page.

Campsite descriptions

We aim to convey an idea of its general appearance, 'feel' and features, with details of pitch numbers, electricity, hardstandings etc.

Facilities

We list specific information on the site's facilities and amenities and, where available, the dates when these facilities are open (if not for the whole season). Much of this information is as supplied to us and may be subject to change. Should any particular activity or aspect of the campsite be important to you, it is always worth discussing with the campsite before you travel.

Swimming pools

Opening dates, any charges and levels of supervision are provided where we have been notified. In some countries (notably France) there is a regulation whereby Bermuda-style shorts may not be worn in swimming pools (for health and hygiene reasons). It is worth ensuring that you do take 'proper' swimming trunks with you.

Charges

Those given are the latest provided to us, usually 2011 prices, and should be viewed as a guide only.

Toilet blocks

We assume that toilet blocks will be equipped with a reasonable number of British style WCs, washbasins and hot showers in cubicles. We also assume that there will be an identified chemical toilet disposal point, and that the campsite will provide water and waste water drainage points and bin areas. If not the case, we comment. We do mention certain features that some readers find important: washbasins in cubicles, facilities for babies, facilities for those with disabilities and motorcaravan service points.

Reservations

Necessary for high season (roughly mid-July to mid-August) in popular holiday areas (i.e. beach resorts). You can reserve many sites via our own Alan Rogers Travel Service or through other tour operators. Remember, many sites are closed all winter and you may struggle to get an answer.

Telephone numbers

All numbers assume that you are phoning from within the country in question. From the UK or Ireland, dial 00, then the country's prefix (e.g. France is 33), then the campsite number given, but dropping the first '0'.

Opening dates

Dates given are those provided to us and can alter before the start of the season. If you intend to visit shortly after a published opening date, or shortly before the closing date, it is wise to check that it will actually be open at the time required. Similarly, some sites operate a restricted service during the low season, only opening some of their facilities (e.g. swimming pools) during the main season; where we know about this, and have the relevant dates, we indicate it – again if you are at all doubtful it is wise to check.

Accommodation

Over recent years, more and more campsites have added high quality mobile homes, chalets, lodges, gites and more. Where applicable we indicate what is available and you'll find details online.

Special Offers

Some campsites have taken the opportunity to highlight a special offer. This is arranged by them and for clarification please contact the campsite direct.

The call of the
great **outdoors**

Campsites across Europe offer a huge range of outdoor activities, and this is the guide to help you find them. You may be a keen mountain biker or windsurfer; you may fancy trying white water rafting or sand yachting during your holiday; or you might simply be looking for a range of exciting activities for the kids this summer (away from the computer screen!).

Either way, there are campsites across Europe offering a chance to enjoy your chosen activity, or try something new. Get out there and give it a try!

Choosing campsites
for outdoor activities

The quality of sporting activities offered by campsites is often remarkable but it's clear that it is no longer enough for a well-run campsite to offer the bare minimum – proper investment, modern infrastructure, quality equipment and qualified professional supervision are all essential.

Convenience and choice

Some campsites offer a wide range of quality activities, aiming for wide appeal to all age groups and interests. This kind of campsite can be a great idea for families with different ages to cater for.

- Camping Ty Nadan in Brittany is exemplary, offering quad biking, aerial zip wires and tree top adventure trails, mountain biking, archery, paintballing and sea kayak excursions.

A specific speciality

Other campsites have become expert in a specific activity, perhaps by virtue of location or personal interest of the owner.

- Camping Wulfener Hals in northern Germany, is ideal for sailing and water sports.

- Camping l'Escale in the French Alps is a great base for a winter sports holiday.

- Camping Jungfrau in Switzerland, is ideal for climbing activities.

- Camping Seiser Alm in the Italian Dolomites and Glen Nevis Caravan and Camping Park in Scotland are great bases for mountain pursuits.

Regional specialities

Some people choose their campsite with a particular activity in mind.

- The lakes of the Landes in southwest France offer superb conditions for windsurfing.

- Many waterside campsites in Holland are popular with sailors for their facilities.

Something
for **everyone**

Swimming

Most family campsites these days boast a swimming pool, often
an impressive aqua park with slides and pools. But for that 'at one
with nature' feel, you can't beat splashing around in a river or lake.
Try the tumbling waters of the Ardeche, with pebbly beaches and
buzzards wheeling overhead above the craggy cliffs. Or enjoy the
cool expanse of inviting waters of a shimmering English lake.

Adventure underground

Some campsites, especially in the Belgian Ardennes, are well
placed for underground activities involving caves, potholes, ropes
and flashlights.

Up in the trees...

A relatively recent innovation are aerial adventure parks, built up in the treetops of mature woodland. Increasing numbers of campsites have their own (le Ty Nadan in Brittany).

Riding

Some campsites, like la Garangeoire in the Vendée, have their own stables and offer riding for all levels. Many others are close by riding facilities.

Canoeing

Canoeing is a great activity on many French campsites, especially in the Ardeche and Dordogne: it's easy to paddle downstream and fun for all the family. Some campsites offer proper tuition, then set you off with lunch and waterproof containers, arranging to meet you downstream and return you to the campsite by minibus.

Watersports

Many campsites are well placed for sailing and windsurfing, some even have their own dinghy launching slipways. Others offer more esoteric activities like kite surfing, scuba diving and water skiing.

Skiing

Skiing is always popular and a little snow should never stop anyone from enjoying a camping holiday! A number of Alpine campsites in France, Austria, and Scandinavia, are open all year round and offer great skiing and snowboarding. Essentials like ski passes and equipment hire are often available while specially adapted mobile homes and accommodation are the norm.

Bikes

Road cycling is hugely popular and easily enjoyed while staying on a campsite. Off road trails for mountain bikes can be found, for example, at Natterersee in the Austrian Tirol.

'Experiences'

Of course, activities can be full-on adrenalin rushes or rather more sedate affairs. A majestic hot air balloon ride over the Loire chateaux, a dawn microlight flight or even an open air painting workshop make for a wonderful and memorable holiday experience.

Outdoor activities for
active **children**

Of course, children enjoy camping holidays at various levels. They enjoy the thrill of sleeping in a different environment; the freedom and fun; and all the small pleasures of being outdoors: pond dipping, watching wildlife, eating breakfast outside every morning. Activities do not always have to be organised.

Children's **Clubs**

Many campsites operate kids' clubs in high season, usually free of charge and multi-national. Activities depend very much on age groups but usually include face painting, treasure hunts, rounders, swimming, circus skills and the like. Activities for older children might include paid-for canoe excursions, bike rides and discos and even rehearsals for a stage show in front of parents at the end of the week.

Qualified instruction...

It's not just the range of activities that is so impressive, it's the degree of professionalism of many campsites. Safety is taken seriously, with appropriate equipment and instruction.

Enjoy...!

Whether you're an 'old hand' or are contemplating your first trip, a regular reader of our Guides or a new 'convert', we wish you well in your travels and hope we have been able to help in some way. We are, of course, also out and about ourselves, visiting sites, talking to owners and readers, and generally checking on standards and new developments. We hope to bump into you!

Wishing you thoroughly enjoyable camping and caravanning in 2012 – favoured by good weather of course!

The Alan Rogers Team

Further **information**

And before you go...

Everyone has different expectations when it comes to holiday activities. And on holiday no-one wants nasty surprises. So be sure to check with the campsite that the activities offered are to your liking before you book.

Insurance

You will naturally have arranged travel insurance for your holiday (and if not, feel free to ask about our own Alan Rogers insurance on 01580 214006 or visit **www.alanrogers.com/travelinsurance**). If planning any dangerous activities please be sure you have appropriate cover.

SPAIN – Sant Pere Pescador

Camping La Gaviota

Ctra de la Platja s/n, E-17470 Sant Pere Pescador (Girona)
t: **972 520 569** e: **info@lagaviota.com**
alanrogers.com/ES80310 www.lagaviota.com

Accommodation: ☑Pitch ☑Mobile home/chalet ☐ Hotel/B&B ☐ Apartment

La Gaviota is a delightful, small, family-run site at the end of a cul-de-sac with direct beach access. This ensures a peaceful situation with a choice of the pleasant L-shaped pool or the fine clean beach with slowly shelving access to the water. Everything here is clean and smart and the Gil family are very keen that you enjoy your time here. There are 165 touring pitches on flat ground with shade and 6A electricity supply. A lush green feel is given to the site by many palms and other semi-tropical trees and shrubs. The restaurant and bar are very pleasant indeed and have a distinct Spanish flavour. The cuisine is reasonably priced, perfectly prepared and served by friendly staff. All facilities are at the reception end of this rectangular site with extra washing up areas at the far end. The guests here were happy and enjoying themselves when we visited. English is spoken here.

You might like to know

Sant Pere Pescador is an outstanding destination for windsurfers and kite surfers thanks to the Tramuntana and Garbí winds.

- ☑ Riding
- ☑ Tennis
- ☑ Cycling *(road)*
- ☑ Outdoor pool
- ☑ Crafts
- ☑ Sailing
- ☑ Windsurfing
- ☑ Kite surfing
- ☑ Diving
- ☑ Golf
- ☑ Kayaking
- ☑ Go-karting
- ☑ Fishing

Facilities: One smart and very clean toilet block is near reception. All WCs are British style and the showers are excellent. Superb facilities for disabled visitors. Two great family rooms plus two baby rooms. Washing machine. Gas supplies. Supermarket (fresh bread), pleasant bar and small, delightful restaurant (all March-Oct). Swimming pool (May-Oct). Playground. Games room. Limited animation. Beach sports and windsurfing. Internet. Torches useful. ATM. Off site: Boat launching 2 km. Riding 4 km. Golf 15 km. Boat excursions. Cycling routes.

Open: 25 March - 30 October.

Directions: From the AP7/E15 take exit 3 onto the N11 north towards Figueras and then the C260 towards Roses. At Castello d'Empúries take the GIV 6216 and continue to Sant Pere Pescador. Site is well signed in the town. GPS: 42.18901, 3.10843

Charges guide

Per unit incl. 2 persons and electricity	€ 23,95 - € 51,95
extra person	€ 3,50 - € 4,50
child (under 10 yrs)	€ 1,50 - € 3,00
dog	€ 2,00 - € 4,00

No credit cards.

Camping Las Palmeras

Ctra de la Platja, E-17470 Sant Pere Pescador (Girona)
t: **972 520 506** e: **info@campinglaspalmeras.com**
alanrogers.com/ES80330 www.campinglaspalmeras.com

Accommodation: ☑ Pitch ☑ Mobile home/chalet ☐ Hotel/B&B ☐ Apartment

A very polished site, the pleasant experience begins as you enter the palm bedecked site and are welcomed at the airy reception building. The 230 pitches are flat, very clean and well maintained, with some shade and 10A electricity. A few pitches are complete with water and drainage. Thirty smart mobile homes are placed unobtrusively around the site. A very pleasant pool complex has a lifeguard and the brightly coloured play areas are clean and safe. A great beach is just a 200 m. walk through a gate at the rear of the site. A full activities programme for children allows parents a break during the day and there is organised fun in the evenings in high season. Full recreational facilities include a gym. The Spanish style restaurant serves high quality food. The owner, Juan Carlos Alcantara, and his wife have many years experience in the campsite business which is clearly demonstrated. You will enjoy your stay here as there is a very happy atmosphere.

You might like to know
Las Palmeras is adjacent to the Punta de la Mora Natural Park, a great area for walking and cycling.

- ☑ Riding
- ☑ Tennis
- ☑ Cycling *(road)*
- ☑ Outdoor pool
- ☑ Crafts
- ☑ Sailing
- ☑ Windsurfing
- ☑ Kite surfing
- ☑ Diving
- ☑ Waterskiing

- ☑ Golf
- ☑ Paintball
- ☑ Hiking
- ☑ Fitness/gym
- ☑ Go-karting

Facilities: Two excellent, very clean, solar powered toilet blocks include first class facilities for disabled campers. Baby rooms. Facilities may become a little busy at peak periods. Washing machines. Motorcaravan services. Supermarket. Restaurant/bar (children's menu). Swimming pools (heated). Play areas. Tennis. five-a-side. Fronton. Boules. Gym. Barbecue. Bicycle hire. Miniclub. Entertainment. Satellite TV. Internet access and WiFi. ATM. Torches useful. Off site: Beach and fishing 200 m. Sailing and boat launching 2 km. Riding 4 km. Golf 7 km.

Open: 27 March - 23 October.

Directions: Sant Pere Pescador is south of Perpignan on coast between Roses and L'Escala. From the AP7/E15 take exit 4 onto the N11 north towards Figueres and then C31 towards Torroella de Fluvia. Take Vilamacolum road east and continue to Sant Pere Pescador. Site well signed in town. GPS: 42.18805, 3.1027

Charges guide

Per unit incl. 2 persons and electricity	€ 23,80 - € 49,90
extra person	€ 3,00 - € 4,30
child (2-9 yrs)	€ 1,70 - € 2,50
dog	free - € 4,30

No credit cards.

SPAIN – Sant Pere Pescador

Camping Las Dunas

Ctra San Marti - Sant Pere, E-17470 Sant Pere Pescador (Girona)
t: **972 521 717** e: **info@campinglasdunas.com**
alanrogers.com/ES80400 **www.campinglasdunas.com**

Accommodation: ☑Pitch ☑Mobile home/chalet ☐ Hotel/B&B ☐ Apartment

Las Dunas is an extremely large, impressive and well-organised resort style site with many on-site activities and an ongoing programme of improvements. It has direct access to a superb sandy beach that stretches along the site for nearly a kilometre with a windsurfing school and beach bar. There is also a much used, huge swimming pool, plus a large double pool for children. Las Dunas is very large, with 1,700 individual hedged pitches (1,479 for tourers) of around 100 sq.m. laid out on flat ground in long, regular parallel rows. All have electricity (6/10A) and 180 also have water and drainage. Shade is available in some parts of the site. Pitches are usually available, even in the main season. Much effort has gone into planting palms and new trees here and the results are very attractive. The large restaurant and bar have spacious terraces overlooking the swimming pools and you can also enjoy a very pleasant, more secluded, cavern style pub. A member of Leading Campings Group.

You might like to know

Las Dunas offers sports competitions, games and other activities organised by a team of professional entertainers.

☑ Riding
☑ Tennis
☑ Cycling *(road)*
☑ Cycling *(mountain biking)*
☑ Sports field
☑ Outdoor pool
☑ Crafts
☑ Archery
☑ Sailing
☑ Windsurfing

☑ Kitesurfing
☑ Diving
☑ Waterskiing
☑ Hiking
☑ Kayaking

Facilities: Five excellent large toilet blocks with British style toilets but no seats, controllable hot showers and washbasins in cabins. Excellent facilities for babies and disabled campers. Laundry facilities. Motorcaravan services. Supermarket and other shops. Large bar with terrace. Large restaurant. Takeaway. Ice cream parlour. Beach bar (main season). Disco club. Swimming pools. Playgrounds. Tennis. Archery. Minigolf. Sailing/windsurfing school. Entertainment/activity programme (15/6-31/8). Exchange facilities. ATM. Safety deposit. Internet café. WiFi. Torches required in some areas. Off site: Resort of L'Escala 5 km. Riding and boat launching 5 km. Water park 10 km. Golf 30 km.

Open: 19 May - 2 September.

Directions: L'Escala is northeast of Girona on the coast between Palamós and Roses. From A7/E15 autostrada take exit 5 towards L'Escala on GI 623. Turn north 2 km. before reaching L'Escala towards Sant Marti d'Ampúrias. Site well signed. GPS: 42.16098, 3.13478

Charges guide

Per unit incl. 2 persons and electricity	€ 21,00 - € 59,20
extra person	€ 3,50 - € 5,75
child (3-10 yrs)	€ 3,00 - € 3,25

Camping Internacional de Calonge

Ctra San Feliu/Guixols - Palamós km 7.6, E-17251 Calonge (Girona)
t: **972 651 233** e: **info@intercalonge.com**
alanrogers.com/ES81300 www.intercalonge.com

Accommodation: ☑ Pitch ☑ Mobile home/chalet ☐ Hotel/B&B ☐ Apartment

This spacious, well laid out site has access to a fine beach via a footbridge over the coast road, or you can take the little road train as the site is on very sloping ground. Calonge is a family site with two good sized pools on different levels, a paddling pool and large sunbathing areas. A great restaurant, bar and snack bar are by the pool. The site's 793 pitches are on terraces and all have electricity (5A), with 84 being fully serviced. The pitches are set on attractively landscaped terraces (access to some may be challenging). There is good shade from the tall pine trees and some views of the sea through the foliage. The upper levels are taken by a tour operator and mobile home pitches. The pools are overlooked by the restaurant terraces which have great views over the mountains. A separate area within the site is set aside for visitors with dogs (including a dog shower!) A nature area within the site is used for walks and picnics. The beach is accessed over the main road by 100 steps, and shared with another campsite.

Special offers
For 2012 special offers (1/1-30/6 and 25/8-31/12) please contact the site.

You might like to know
A special weekly programme is available in collaboration with Tennis World at Platja d'Aro, including friendship games with club members.

☑ Riding
☑ Pony trekking
☑ Tennis
☑ Cycling (road)
☑ Cycling (mountain biking)
☑ Sports field
☑ Outdoor pool
☑ Crafts
☑ Sailing
☑ Surfing

☑ Windsurfing
☑ Diving
☑ Golf
☑ Hiking
☑ Kayaking

Facilities: New and renovated toilet blocks (one heated in winter) include some washbasins in cabins. No toilet seats. Laundry facilities. Motorcaravan services. Gas supplies. Shop (26/3-30/10), Restaurant (1/2-31/12). Bar. Patio bar with pizzas and takeaway (27/3-24/10, then weekends). Swimming pools (26/3-16/10). Playground. Electronic games. Rather noisy disco two nights a week (but not late). Bicycle hire. Tennis. Hairdresser. ATM. Internet access and WiFi. Torches necessary in some areas. Road train from the bottom of the site to the top in high season. Off site: Bus at the gate. Fishing 300 m. Supermarket 500 m. Golf 3 km. Riding 10 km.

Open: All year.

Directions: Site is on the inland side of the coast road between Palamós and Platja d'Aro. Take the C31 south to the 661 at Calonge. At Calonge follow signs to the C253 towards Platja d'Aro and on to site. GPS: 41.83333, 3.08417

Charges guide

Per unit incl. 2 persons and electricity	€ 20,25 - € 47,70
extra person	€ 3,70 - € 8,35
child (3-10 yrs)	€ 1,85 - € 4,55
dog	€ 3,30 - € 4,30

No credit cards.

Camping Roche

N340 km 19,5, Carril de Pilahito, E-11140 Conil de la Frontera (Cádiz)
t: 956 442 216 e: info@campingroche.com
alanrogers.com/ES88590 www.campingroche.com

Accommodation: ☑ Pitch ☑ Mobile home/chalet ☐ Hotel/B&B ☐ Apartment

Camping Roche is situated in a pine forest near white sandy beaches in the lovely region of Andalucia. It is a clean, tidy and welcoming site. English is spoken but try your Spanish, German or French as the staff are very helpful. A family site, it offers a variety of facilities including a sports area and swimming pools. The restaurant has good food and a pleasant outlook over the pool. Games are organised for children. A recently built extension provides further pitches, a new toilet block and a tennis court. There are 335 pitches which include 104 bungalows to rent. The touring pitches all have electricity (10A), and 76 also have water and waste water. There are pleasant paths in the area for mountain biking and this is an ideal base for visiting the cities of Seville and Cádiz.

You might like to know
The cities of Seville and Cádiz are both within easy reach for day trips.

- ☑ Riding
- ☑ Pony trekking
- ☑ Tennis
- ☑ Cycling (road)
- ☑ Sports field
- ☑ Outdoor pool
- ☑ Sailing
- ☑ Surfing
- ☑ Windsurfing
- ☑ Kitesurfing

- ☑ Diving
- ☑ Golf
- ☑ Hiking
- ☑ Fitness/gym
- ☑ Fishing

Facilities: Three toilet blocks are traditional in style and provide simple, clean facilities. Washbasins have cold water only. Washing machine. Supermarket. Bar and restaurant. Swimming and paddling pools. Sports area. Tennis. Play area. Off site: Bus stops 3 times daily outside gates. Cádiz. Cape Trafalgar. Baelo Claudia archaeological site.

Open: All year.

Directions: From the N340 (Cádiz - Algeciras) turn off to site at km. 19.5 point. From Conil, take El Pradillo road. Keep following signs to site. From CA3208 road turn at km. 1 and site is 1.5 km. down this road on the right.
GPS: 36.31089, -6.11268

Charges guide

Per unit incl. 2 persons and electricity	€ 18,81 - € 33,10
extra person	€ 3,71 - € 6,50
child	€ 3,14 - € 5,50
dog	€ 2,14 - € 3,75

Camping Picos de Europa

E-33556 Avín-Onís (Asturias)
t: 985 844 070 e: info@picos-europa.com
alanrogers.com/ES89650 www.picos-europa.com

Accommodation: ☑ Pitch ☑ Mobile home/chalet ☐ Hotel/B&B ☑ Apartment

This delightful site is, as its name suggests, an ideal spot from which to explore these dramatic limestone mountains on foot, by bicycle or on horseback. The site itself is continuously developing and the dynamic owner, José, and his nephew who helps out when he is away, are both very pleasant and nothing is too much trouble. The site is in a valley beside a pleasant, fast flowing river. The 160 marked pitches are of varying sizes and have been developed in three avenues, on level grass mostly backing on to hedging, with 6A electricity. An area for tents and apartments is over a bridge past the fairly small, but pleasant, round swimming pool. Local stone has been used for the L-shaped building at the main entrance which houses reception and a very good bar/restaurant. The site can organise caving activities, and has information about the Cares gorge along with the many energetic ways of exploring the area, including by canoe and quad-bike! The Bulnes funicular railway is well worth a visit.

You might like to know

White-water canoeing at the Sella descent has different starting points, providing courses from 6 km. to 14 km. One- two- and three-seat canoes are available.

- ☑ Riding
- ☑ Cycling (mountain biking)
- ☑ Outdoor pool
- ☑ Rafting
- ☑ Canyoning
- ☑ Potholing
- ☑ Hiking
- ☑ Aerial walkways
- ☑ Canoeing
- ☑ Kayaking

Facilities: Toilet facilities include a new fully equipped block, along with new facilities for disabled visitors and babies. Pleasant room with tables and chairs for poor weather. Washing machine and dryer. Shop (July-Sept). Swimming pool (Feb-Sept). Bar and cafeteria style restaurant (all year) serves a good value 'menu del dia' and snacks. WiFi in restaurant area. Play area. Fishing. Torches necessary in the new tent area. Off site: Riding 12 km. Bicycle hire 15 km. Golf and coast at Llanes 25 km.

Open: All year.

Directions: Avín is 15 km. east of Cangas de Onís on AS114 road to Panes and is probably best approached from this direction especially if towing. From A8 (Santander - Oviedo) use km. 326 exit and N634 northwest to Arriondas. Turn southeast on N625 to Cangas and join the AS114 (Covodonga/Panes) by-passing Cangas. Site is just beyond Avín after 16 km. marker. GPS: 43.3363, -4.94498

Charges guide

Per person	€ 5,02
child (under 14 yrs)	€ 4,01
pitch incl. car	€ 8,57 - € 9,64
electricity	€ 3,75

Orbitur Camping Rio Alto

EN13 km 13 Rio Alto-Est, Estela, P-4570-275 Póvoa de Varzim (Porto)
t: 252 615 699 e: inforioalto@orbitur.pt
alanrogers.com/PO8030 www.orbitur.pt

Accommodation: ☑Pitch ☑Mobile home/chalet ☐ Hotel/B&B ☐ Apartment

This site makes an excellent base for visiting Porto which is some 35 km. south of Estela. It has around 700 pitches on sandy terrain and is next to what is virtually a private beach. There are some hardstandings for caravans and motorcaravans and electrical connections to most pitches (long leads may be required). The area for tents is furthest from the beach and windswept, stunted pines give some shade. There are arrangements for car parking away from camping areas in peak season. There is a quality restaurant, a snack bar and a large swimming pool across the road from reception. An 18-hole golf course is adjacent and huge nets along one side of the site protect campers from any stray balls. The beach is accessed via a novel double tunnel in two lengths of 40 metres beneath the dunes (open 09.00-19.00). The beach shelves steeply at some tidal stages (lifeguard 15/6-15/9).

You might like to know

The first European campsite to be certified for service quality standards by SGS ICS. Rio Alto has direct access to a fine beach, via a tunnel beneath a golf course in the heart of Portugal's Green Coast.

- ☑ Riding
- ☑ Tennis
- ☑ Cycling (road)
- ☑ Sports field
- ☑ Outdoor pool
- ☑ Sailing
- ☑ Windsurfing
- ☑ Golf
- ☑ Kayaking
- ☑ Fishing

Facilities: Four refurbished and well equipped toilet blocks have hot water. Laundry facilities. Facilities for disabled campers. Gas supplies. Shop (1/6-31/10). Restaurant, bar, snack bar (1/5-31/10). Swimming pool (1/6-30/9). Tennis. Playground. Games room. Surfing. TV. Medical post. Car wash. Evening entertainment twice weekly in season. Off site: Fishing. Golf. Bicycle hire. Riding (all within 5 km).

Open: All year.

Directions: From A28 in direction of Porto, leave at exit 18 signed Fao/Apuila. At roundabout take N13 in direction of Pavoa de Varzim/Porto for 2.5 km. At Hotel Contriz, turn right onto narrow cobbled road. Site well signed in 2 km.
GPS: 41.44504, -8.75767

Charges guide

Per person	€ 2,90 - € 5,40
child (5-10 yrs)	€ 1,50 - € 3,00
caravan and car	€ 6,80 - € 12,00
electricity (5/15A)	€ 2,50 - € 3,10

PORTUGAL – Odemira

Zmar-Eco Camping Resort

Herdade ç de Mateus E.N. 393/1, San Salvador, P-7630 Odemira (Beja)
t: **707 200 626** e: **info@zmar.eu**
alanrogers.com/PO8175 www.zmar.eu

Accommodation: ☑Pitch ☑Mobile home/chalet ☐ Hotel/B&B ☐ Apartment

Zmar is an exciting new project which should be fully open this year. The site is located near Zambujeira do Mar, on the Alentejo coast. This is a highly ambitious initiative developed along very strict environmental lines. For example, renewable resources such as locally harvested timber and recycled plastic are used wherever possible and solar energy is used whenever practicable. Public indoor spaces have no air conditioning, but there is adequate cooling through underfloor ventilation and electric fans where possible. Pitches are 100 sq.m. and benefit from artificial shade. Caravans and wood-clad mobile homes are also available for rent. The swimming pool complex features a large outdoor pool and an indoor pool area with a wave machine and a wellness centre. The very large and innovative children's play park has climbing nets, labyrinths and caves. There is also a children's farm and a large play house. For adults, many sporting amenities will be available around the resort's 81 hectare park.

You might like to know
On the campsite you will find a Centre for Environmental Interpretation describing the fauna, flora and climate of the region, and displaying a selection of historical artefacts.

☑ **Tennis**
☑ **Cycling** (mountain biking)
☑ **Sports field**
☑ **Outdoor pool**
☑ **Archery**
☑ **Hiking**
☑ **Canoeing**
☑ **Fitness/gym**
☑ **Fishing**
☑ **Treetop Adventures**

Facilities: Eight toilet blocks provide comprehensive facilities including those for children and disabled visitors. Bar. Restaurant. Crêperie. Takeaway food. Large supermarket. Swimming pool. Covered pool. Wellness centre. Sports field. Games room. Play area, farm and play house. Tennis. Bicycle hire. Activity and entertainment programme. Mobile homes and caravans for rent. Caravan repair and servicing. The site's own debit card system is used for payment at all facilities. Off site: Vicentina coast and the Alentejo Natural Park. Sines (birthplace of Vasco de Gama). Cycle and walking tracks. Sea fishing.

Open: All year.

Directions: From the N120 from Odemira to Lagos, at roundabout in the centre of Portas de Transval turn towards Milfontes. Take turn to Cabo Sardão and then Zambujeira do Mar. Site is on the left. GPS: 37.60422, -8.73142

Charges guide

Per unit incl. up to 4 persons and electricity	€ 20,00 - € 50,00
extra person	€ 5,00 - € 10,00
child (4-12 yrs)	€ 5,00

ITALY – Dimaro

Dolomiti Camping Village

Via Gole 105, I-38025 Dimaro (Trentino - Alto Adige)
t: **0463 974 332** e: info@campingdolomiti.com
alanrogers.com/IT61830 www.campingdolomiti.com

Accommodation: ☑Pitch ☑Mobile home/chalet ☐ Hotel/B&B ☐ Apartment

Dolomiti di Brenta is open for separate winter and summer seasons. It is situated at an altitude of 800 m. in an attractive, open valley surrounded by the rugged Dolomite Mountains, and is only 100 m. from the River Noce. It is an ideal base to explore this fantastic region. There are 195 level and grassy pitches, all with 4A electricity and some fully serviced. Young trees offer a little shade. The pitches range in size from small (45 sq.m), suitable for small tents, to large (100 sq.m) suitable for medium sized outfits. The Dolomites are one of the most spectacular unspoilt mountain regions of Europe and it is easy to go off the beaten track and find some real peace and quiet. It is close to the Estelvio National Park, the largest in Italy and home to a wide variety of flora and fauna. The area can be explored on foot, by mountain bike or in the car, and energetic families can enjoy a wide range of activities on the river and in the surrounding mountains.

Facilities: Modern toilet block with all necessary facilities including private bathrooms for rent. Washing machine, dryer. Small shop. Bar, restaurant, pizzeria. Outdoor swimming pool and spa. Fitness centre. Large children's play area. Communal barbecues. Football. Volleyball. WiFi. Off site: Attractive mountain villages with their local craft shops and the Estelvio national park. Many marked hiking and biking trails. Shops, bars, restaurant and swimming pool in Malè.

Open: 4 December - 10 April,
21 May - 25 September.

Directions: Leave the A22, Brenner motorway at San Michele All'Adige, about 40 km. south of Bolzano. Follow signs for SS43 through Cles, then SS42 through Malè. 19 km. after Cles turn left in Via Gole, site is on right.
GPS: 46.325278, 10.863056

Charges guide

Per unit incl. 2 persons and electricity	€ 26,40 - € 42,70
dog (not July/Aug)	€ 3,00 - € 4,00

Special offers
Two-night camping stay with spa entrance, 30-minute massage, pool and outdoor sports: € 155/person.

You might like to know
The campsite is located between two different national parks and within easy reach of the Brenta Dolomites – ideal for trekking, mountain-biking, rafting and skiing.

☑ Riding
☑ Cycling *(road)*
☑ Cycling *(mountain biking)*
☑ Outdoor pool
☑ Golf
☑ Rafting
☑ Canyoning
☑ Rock climbing
☑ Hiking
☑ Skiing *(downhill)*

☑ Snowboarding
☑ Kayaking
☑ Tennis
☑ Cross-country skiing

ITALY – Lana

Camping Arquin

Feldgatterweg 25, I-39011 Lana (Trentino - Alto Adige)
t: 0473 561 187   e: info@camping-arquin.it
alanrogers.com/IT61865   www.camping-arquin.it

Accommodation: ☑Pitch ☑Mobile home/chalet ☐ Hotel/B&B ☐ Apartment

Camping Arquin is in the South Tirol (Alto Adige) where the majority of the population speak German. It is open from early March to mid November and lies in an open valley surrounded by orchards, beyond which are high mountains. This is a region of natural beauty and is famous for its flowery meadows. The site is close to the village of Lana, one of the largest in the South Tyrol and famous for its Mediterranean climate. There are 120 small, sunny, level, grass pitches all with 6A electricity and many are fully serviced. There is a wide range of marked footpaths and cycling routes. This is a good base for active families wishing to explore the local area on foot, by bicycle, in the car, by bus or by train. The higher reaches of the mountains can be accessed by cable car. This area is also known for its thermal springs and baths. The interesting old town of Meran is only 7 km. and is accessible by bus.

Special offers
Campsite guests benefit from free access to the public swimming pool in Lana.

You might like to know
Some of the great names of the Dolomites are within easy reach, including Cortina d'Ampezzo and Seiseralm.

☑ Tennis
☑ Cycling (road)
☑ Cycling (mountain biking)
☑ Outdoor pool
☑ Golf
☑ Rock climbing
☑ Hiking
☑ Canoeing
☑ Fishing

Facilities: Modern toilet block with all necessary facilities including those for babies and disabled visitors. Motorcaravan services. Small shop. Restaurant and bar. Small swimming pool. Children's play area. Internet point. Off site: Bus stop 200 m. Large swimming pool 200 m. (May onwards; free to campers). Historical town of Meran 7 km. Museums. Golf. Biking. Hiking. Tennis. Paragliding. Rock climbing. Canoeing. Nature parks. Cable car.

Open: 1 March - 15 November.

Directions: Leave A22 Brenner motorway at Bozen Süd. Take expressway towards Meran. At the Lana-Burgstall exit turn left. After 250 m. take first right and follow signs to site. GPS: 46.611151, 11.174434

Charges guide

Per unit incl. 2 persons and electricity	€ 30,00 - € 34,00
dog	free

26

ITALY – Rasen

Camping Corones

I-39030 Rasen (Trentino - Alto Adige)
t: 047 449 6490 e: info@corones.com
alanrogers.com/IT61990 www.corones.com

Accommodation: ☑Pitch ☑Mobile home/chalet ☐ Hotel/B&B ☑ Apartment

Situated in a pine forest clearing at the foot of the attractive Antholz valley in the heart of German-speaking Südtirol, Camping Corones is ideally situated both for winter sports enthusiasts and for walkers, cyclists, mountain bikers and those who prefer to explore the valleys and mountain roads of the Dolomites by car. There are 135 level pitches, all with electricity (16A) and many also with water, drainage and satellite TV. The Residence offers luxury apartments, and there are authentic Canadian log cabins for hire. The bar/restaurant and small shop are open all season. From the site you can see slopes, which in winter become highly rated skiing pistes. A short drive up the broad Antholz (Anterselva) valley takes you to an internationally important biathlon centre. An excellent day trip would be to drive up the valley and over the pass into Austria. Back on site, a small pool and paddling pool could be very welcome. There is a regular programme of free excursions and occasional evening events are organised.

Special offers
Free Skibus. Family deals. 'White weeks'.

You might like to know
There are plenty of activities on site, with something for everyone – tranquil spots for those wanting to relax in the fresh air, and many opportunities for those seeking activities and adventure. There is a children's activity programme in summer.

☑ Riding
☑ Tennis
☑ Golf
☑ Rock climbing
☑ Hiking
☑ Skiing *(downhill)*
☑ Skiing *(cross-country)*
☑ Snowboarding
☑ Aerial walkways
☑ Climbing wall

☑ Guided walks
☑ Ski safari
☑ Snowshoeing
☑ Road/offroad cycling
☑ Fishing

Facilities: The central toilet block is traditional but well maintained and clean. Additional facilities below the Residence are of the highest quality including individual shower rooms with washbasins, washbasins with all WCs, and facilities for children and disabled visitors. Fully equipped private shower rooms for hire. Luxurious wellness centre with saunas, solarium, jacuzzis, massage, therapy pools and heat benches. Heated outdoor swimming and paddling pools. Play area. Internet facilities. Off site: Tennis 800 m. Bicycle hire 1 km. Riding and fishing 3 km. Golf (9 holes) 10 km.

Open: 6 December - 30 March,
31 May - 31 October.

Directions: Rasen/Rasun is 85 km. northeast of Bolzano. From Bressanone/Brixen exit on A22 Brenner-Modena motorway, go east on SS49 for 50 km. then turn north (signed Rasen/Antholz). Turn immediately west at roundabout in Niederrasen/Rasun di Sotto to site on left in 100 m. GPS: 46.7758, 12.0367

Charges guide

Per unit incl. 2 persons, electricity on meter	€ 19,70 - € 28,80
extra person	€ 4,60 - € 7,80
child (3-15 yrs)	€ 3,00 - € 7,20

Caravan Park Sexten

Saint Josef Strasse 54, I-39030 Sexten (Trentino - Alto Adige)
t: 047 471 0444 e: info@caravanparksexten.it
alanrogers.com/IT62030 www.caravanparksexten.it

Accommodation: ☑Pitch ☑Mobile home/chalet ☐ Hotel/B&B ☐ Apartment

Caravan Park Sexten is 1,520 metres above sea level and has 268 pitches, some very large and all with electricity (16A), TV connections and water and drainage in summer and winter (underground heating stops pipes freezing). Some pitches are in the open to catch the sun, others are tucked in forest clearings by the river. They are mostly gravelled to provide an ideal all-year surface. It is the facilities that make this a truly remarkable site; no expense or effort has been spared to create a luxurious environment that matches that of any top class hotel. The health spa has every type of sauna, Turkish and Roman baths, sunbeds, herbal and hay baths, hairdressing and beauty treatment salons, relaxation and massage rooms and a remarkable indoor pool with children's pool, Kneipp therapy pool and whirlpools. The timber of the buildings is from 400-year-old farmhouses and is blended with top quality modern materials to create amazing interiors and (mainly) authentic Tyrolean exteriors.

You might like to know

You can choose between a day trip to a famous city such as Venice, or to Lake Garda, where you can breathe in both the mountain and the Mediterranean atmosphere.

- ☑ Riding
- ☑ Tennis
- ☑ Cycling (road)
- ☑ Cycling (mountain biking)
- ☑ Sports field
- ☑ Outdoor pool
- ☑ Golf
- ☑ Rock climbing
- ☑ Hiking
- ☑ Skiing (downhill)

- ☑ Skiing (cross-country)
- ☑ Snowboarding
- ☑ Aerial walkways
- ☑ Climbing wall
- ☑ Fitness/gym
- ☑ Fishing

Facilities: The three main toilet blocks have heated floors, controllable showers and hairdryers. Luxurious private facilities to rent. Children and baby rooms. En-suite facilities for disabled visitors. Laundry and drying room. Motorcaravan services. Shop. Bars and restaurants with entertainment 2-3 nights a week. Indoor pool. Heated outdoor pool (1/6-30/9). High quality health spa. New outdoor play area. Good range of activities for all. Tennis. Bicycle hire. Climbing wall. Fishing. Adventure activity packages. Internet access and WiFi (whole site). Off site: Skiing in winter (free bus to 2 ski lifts within 5 km). Walking, cycling and climbing.

Open: All year.

Directions: Sexten/Sesto is 110 km. northeast of Bolzano. From Bressanone/Brixen exit on the A22 Brenner - Modena motorway follow the SS49 east for about 60 km. Turn south on the SS52 at Innichen/San Candido and follow signs to Sexten. Site is 5 km. past village (signed). GPS: 46.66727, 12.40221

Charges guide

Per unit incl. 2 persons	€ 22,00 - € 49,00
extra person	€ 8,00 - € 13,00
child (2-14 yrs)	€ 4,50 - € 11,00
electricity per kWh (16A)	€ 0,70

Camping Seiser Alm

Saint Konstantin 16, I-39050 Völs am Schlern (Trentino - Alto Adige)
t: **047 170 6459** e: **info@camping-seiseralm.com**
alanrogers.com/IT62040 www.camping-seiseralm.com

Accommodation: ☑Pitch ☑Mobile home/chalet ☐ Hotel/B&B ☑ Apartment

What an amazing experience awaits you at Seiser Alm! Elisabeth and Erhard Mahlknecht have created a superb site in the magnificent Südtirol region of the Dolomite mountains. Towering peaks provide a magnificent backdrop when you dine in the charming, traditional style restaurant on the upper terrace. Here you will also find the bar, shop and reception. The 150 touring pitches are of a very high standard with a 16A electricity supply, 120 with gas, water, drainage and satellite connections. Guests were delighted with the site when we visited, many coming to walk or cycle, some just to enjoy the surroundings. There are countless things to see and do here. Enjoy the grand 18-hole golf course alongside the site or join the organised excursions and activities. Local buses and cable cars provide an excellent service for summer visitors and skiers alike (discounts are available). In keeping with the natural setting, the majority of the luxury facilities are set into the hillside.

You might like to know

The Seiser Alm campsite is located in the beautiful landscape surrounding Alpe di Siusi, with a fine view of the towering Sciliar Massif, the symbol of Alto Adige.

- ☑ Riding
- ☑ Pony trekking
- ☑ Tennis
- ☑ Cycling (road)
- ☑ Outdoor pool
- ☑ Crafts
- ☑ Golf
- ☑ Rock climbing
- ☑ Hiking
- ☑ Skiing (downhill)

- ☑ Skiing (cross-country)
- ☑ Snowboarding
- ☑ Aerial walkways
- ☑ Climbing wall
- ☑ Microlighting

Facilities: One luxury underground block is in the centre of the site. 16 private units are available. Excellent facilities for children and disabled visitors. Washing machines and large drying room. Sauna. Supermarket. Quality restaurant and bar with terrace. Entertainment programme. Miniclub. Children's adventure park and play room. Special rooms for ski equipment. Torches useful. WiFi (charged). Apartments and mobile homes for rent. Off site: Riding adjacent. 18-hole golf course (discounts) and fishing 1 km. Bicycle hire and lake swimming 2 km. ATM 3 km. Skiing in winter. Buses to cable cars and ski lifts.

Open: All year excl. 2 November - 20 December.

Directions: Site is east of Bolzano. From the A22/E45 take Bolzano Nord exit. Take road for Prato Isarco/Blumau, then road for Fie/Völs. Take care as the split in the road is sudden. If you miss left fork as you enter a tunnel (Altopiano dello Sciliar-Schlerngebiet) you will pay dearly in extra kilometres. Enjoy climb to Völs am Schlern and site is well signed. GPS: 46.53344, 11.53335

Charges guide

Per unit incl. 2 persons	€ 17,30 - € 43,50
extra person	€ 6,90 - € 9,50
child (2-16 yrs)	€ 3,60 - € 7,70
electricity (per kWh)	€ 0,60

Camping Residence Sägemühle

Dornweg 12, I-39026 Prad am Stilfserjoch (Trentino - Alto Adige)
t: 047 361 6078 e: info@campingsaegemuehle.com
alanrogers.com/IT62070 www.campingsaegemuehle.com

Accommodation: ☑Pitch ☑Mobile home/chalet ☐ Hotel/B&B ☐ Apartment

This very attractive, well maintained site with beautiful mountain views is alongside a little village. The 160 grass touring pitches are neat and level, some have shade and most have electricity, water and drainage. The high standard indoor pool area is welcoming to cool oneself in the summer and relax in warm water after skiing in winter. The excellent facilities are cleverly placed under the pool area. New for the season is an enlarged reception, well equipped gym and a coffee bar with terrace leading to a very good restaurant. There is a new lift for those with mobility problems, although the facilities for disabled visitors are on ground level. Animation is provided in July and August and shared with a sister site. The area is renowned for its winter sports but has much to offer throughout the open season and reception will help with tourist information. The friendly owners speak some English and Dutch.

You might like to know
This is a great base for a winter sports holiday, with toboggan races and a children's ski lift adjacent to the site.

- ☑ Tennis
- ☑ Cycling (road)
- ☑ Cycling (mountain biking)
- ☑ Outdoor pool
- ☑ Golf
- ☑ Rafting
- ☑ Hiking
- ☑ Skiing (downhill)
- ☑ Skiing (cross-country)
- ☑ Fishing

Facilities: The main and very modern sanitary facilities are under the pool complex. All WCs are British style and the showers are of high quality. Private cabins for hire. Facilities for disabled visitors. Children's facilities and baby baths. Washing machines. Restaurant and bar. Coffee bar with terrace. Indoor swimming pool with waves, jacuzzi and waterfall. Gym and sauna. Entertainment programme in season. Miniclub. Play areas. Internet. WiFi throughout (charged). Torches useful. Off site: Town facilities. Natural spring for paddling 800 m. Bicycle hire 300 m. Riding 800 m. Golf 30 km.

Open: All year excl. 8 November - 19 December.

Directions: Site is west of Bolzano. From A38/S40 west of Bolzano, take exit for Pso dello Stelvio/Stilfserjoch (also marked S38) and village of Prad am Stilfserjoch. Site is well signed from here. GPS: 46.617628, 10.595317

Charges guide

Per unit incl. 2 persons and electricity	€ 27,60 - € 41,10
extra person	€ 8,00 - € 11,00
child (2-15 yrs)	€ 5,50 - € 9,00
dog	€ 3,50 - € 5,00

ITALY – Calceranica al Lago

Camping Punta Lago

Via Lungo Lago 42, I-38050 Calceranica al Lago (Trentino - Alto Adige)
t: **046 172 3229** e: **info@campingpuntalago.com**
alanrogers.com/IT62260 www.campingpuntalago.com

Accommodation: ☑ Pitch ☑ Mobile home/chalet ☐ Hotel/B&B ☐ Apartment

Camping Punta Lago is in a beautiful setting on Lago di Caldonazzo. This attractive family run campsite, with easy lake access across a small road, has 140 level, shaded pitches on grass. Of a good size, all have electricity (3/6A) and 50 are serviced with water and drainage. The campsite first opened 45 years ago and brothers Gino and Mauro continue the friendly family tradition of ensuring you enjoy your holiday. As President of 'Consortia Trentino Outdoors', Gino knows all about the range of activities available locally including fishing, lake swimming, windsurfing, sailing and canoeing. There are excellent restaurants within 50 m. of the gate. The site itself has a large terraced snack bar with wonderful views of the lake and the most amazing ice cream (gelato), yogurt and fruit concoctions.

Special offers
Special offers are available for many activities, for example rafting and canyoning. Site visitors receive a Trentino Outdoor Camping Card with special deals on shopping and sporting activities locally.

You might like to know
There is a shelter with all the necessary equipment to maintain your bicycle. Information and demonstrations of things to do in the area are provided for visitors.

☑ Riding
☑ Tennis
☑ Cycling (road)
☑ Cycling (mountain biking)
☑ Sailing
☑ Windsurfing
☑ Hiking
☑ Canoeing
☑ Pedalos
☑ Fishing

☑ Trekking
☑ Nordic walking
☑ Paragliding
☑ Swimming
☑ Orienteering

Facilities: One central sanitary block has superb facilities with hot water throughout. Excellent facilities for disabled visitors and babies. Private units for rent, some with massage baths. Washing machines and dryer. Freezer. Shop. Bar/snack bar. Fishing (with permit). Modern play area. Entertainment programme (July/Aug). Internet access. WiFi throughout (charged). Cinema. TV. Off site: Bicycle hire, town and ATM 1 km. Watersports. Riding 3 km. Golf 20 km. Train 1 km. to Venice and other cities.

Open: 1 May - 15 September.

Directions: From A22 Bolzano - Trento autostrada take the SS47 towards Padova. After about 15 km. turn for Lago di Caldonazzo and Calceranica al Lago. Approaching town from the west beside the railway, continue along Via Donegani, turn left at the Esso petrol station into Via al Lago and right at lakeside into Via Lungo Lago. Site is on right. Coming from the east follow Calceranica then turn right just before Esso petrol station. Do not try to cut across before this as you will enter a one-way system with no through road to site. GPS: 46.00230, 11.25450

Charges guide

Per unit incl. 2 persons and electricity	€ 16,00 - € 40,00
extra person	€ 5,00 - € 9,00

Camping Lago di Levico

Loc. Pleina 5, I-38056 Levico Terme (Trentino - Alto Adige)
t: 046 170 6491   e: info@lagolevico.com
alanrogers.com/IT62290   www.lagolevico.com

Accommodation: ☑ Pitch ☑ Mobile home/chalet ☐ Hotel/B&B ☐ Apartment

Camping Lago di Levico, by a pretty lakeside in the mountains, is the merger of two popular sites, Camping Lévico and Camping Jolly. Brothers Andrea and Geno Antoniolli are making great improvements, already there is an impressive new reception and further developments of the lakeside and swimming areas are planned. The lakeside pitches are quite special. There are 430 mostly grassy and shaded pitches (70-120 sq.m) with 6A electricity, 150 also have water and drainage and 12 have private facilities. Staff are welcoming and fluent in English. The swimming pool complex is popular, as is the summer family entertainment. There is a small supermarket on site and it is a short distance to the local village. The restaurant, bar, pizzeria and takeaway are open all season. The beautiful grass shores of the lake are ideal for sunbathing and the crystal clear water is ideal for enjoying (non-motorised) water activities. This is a site where the natural beauty of an Italian lake is not overwhelmed by commercial tourism.

You might like to know

There is a large private beach. The clear, shallow waters of the lake offer opportunities for swimming, fishing, canoeing, and boating. You can rent canoes and pedal boats at reception.

- ☑ Riding
- ☑ Pony trekking
- ☑ Tennis
- ☑ Sailing
- ☑ Diving
- ☑ Rafting
- ☑ Rock climbing
- ☑ Skiing (downhill)
- ☑ Climbing wall
- ☑ 10-pin bowling
- ☑ Yoga
- ☑ Walking tours
- ☑ Road/off-road cycling
- ☑ Canoeing/boating
- ☑ Water skiing

Facilities: Four modern sanitary blocks with hot water for showers, washbasins and washing. Mostly British style toilets. Single locked unit for disabled visitors. Laundry facilities. Freezer. Motorcaravan service point. Good shop. Bar/restaurant and takeaway. Outdoor swimming pool. Play area. Miniclub and entertainment (high season). Fishing. Satellite TV and cartoon cinema. Internet access (free in low season). Kayak hire. Tennis. Torches useful. Off site: Boat launching 500 m. Bicycle hire and bicycle track 1.5 km. Town with all the usual facilities and ATM 2 km. Riding 3 km. Golf 6 km.

Open: 15 April - 10 October.

Directions: From A22 Verona - Bolzano road take turn for Trento on S47 to Levico Terme where campsite is very well signed.
GPS: 46.00799, 11.28454

Charges guide

Per unit incl. 2 persons and electricity	€ 9,50 - € 38,00
extra person	€ 3,00 - € 14,25
child (3-11 yrs)	free - € 6,50
dog	free - € 5,00

Camping Villaggio dei Fiori

Via Tiro a Volo 3, I-18038 San Remo (Ligúria)
t: **018 466 0635** e: **info@villaggiodeifiori.it**
alanrogers.com/IT64010 www.villaggiodeifiori.it

Accommodation: ☑Pitch ☑Mobile home/chalet ☐ Hotel/B&B ☐ Apartment

Open all year round, this open and spacious site is a member of the Senelia group and maintains very high standards. It is ideal for exploring the Italian and French Rivieras or for just relaxing by the enjoyable, filtered sea water pools or on the private beach. Unusually, all of the pitch areas at the site are totally paved, with some extremely large pitches for large units (ask reception to open another gate for entry). Electricity (3/6A) is available (at extra cost) to all 107 pitches; 20 also have water and drainage, and there is an outside sink and cold water for every four pitches. There is ample shade from mature trees and shrubs, which are constantly watered and cared for in summer. The 'gold' pitches and some wonderful tent pitches are along the seafront with great views. There is a path to a secluded and pleasant beach with sparkling waters, overlooked by a large patio area. The rocky surrounds are excellent for snorkelling and fishing, with ladder access to the water. The friendly management speak excellent English.

You might like to know
Bicycles can be hired on site, and a new cycle track has been developed, along the route of a former railway line.

- ☑ Riding
- ☑ Cycling *(road)*
- ☑ Cycling *(mountain biking)*
- ☑ Outdoor pool
- ☑ Sailing
- ☑ Windsurfing
- ☑ Golf
- ☑ Multisports court
- ☑ Fishing

Facilities: Four clean and modern toilet blocks have British and Turkish style WCs and hot water throughout. Controllable showers. Baby rooms. Facilities for disabled campers. Laundry facilities. Motorcaravan services. Gas. Bar sells limited essential supplies. Large restaurant. Pizzeria and takeaway (all year; prepaid card system). Sea water swimming pools (small extra charge in high season) and heated whirlpool spa (June-Sept). Tennis. Excellent play area. Fishing. Satellite TV. Internet access. WiFi (charged). Bicycle hire. Dogs are not accepted. Off site: Bus at gate. Supermarket 100 m. Shop 150 m. Riding and golf 2 km. Very safe cycle route to the city and a further 24 km. along coastal path.

Open: All year.

Directions: From SS1 (Ventimiglia-Imperia), site is on right just before San Remo. There is a very sharp right turn into site if approaching from the west. From autostrada A10 take San Remo exit. Site is well signed. GPS: 43.80117, 7.74867

Charges guide

Per unit incl. 4 persons and electricity	€ 35,00 - € 72,00

Camping Bled

Kidriceva 10c SI, SLO-4260 Bled
t: 045 752 000   e: info@camping-bled.com
alanrogers.com/SV4200   www.camping-bled.com

Accommodation: ☑ Pitch   ☑ Mobile home/chalet   ☐ Hotel/B&B   ☐ Apartment

On the western tip of Lake Bled is Camping Bled. The waterfront here has a small public beach, immediately behind which runs a gently sloping narrow wooded valley. Pitches at the front, used mainly for overnighters, are now marked, separated by trees and enlarged, bringing the total number to 280. In areas at the back, visitors are free to pitch where they like. There is some noise from trains as they trundle out of a high tunnel overlooking the campsite on the line from Bled to Bohinj. But this is a small price to pay for the pleasure of being in a pleasant site from which the lake, its famous little island, its castle and town can be explored on foot or by boat. Unlike many other Slovenian sites, the number of statics (and semi-statics) here appears to be carefully controlled with touring caravans, motorcaravans and tents predominating.

You might like to know
There are special birdwatching and nature programmes – over 100 nesting places have been set up across the site. Binoculars and brochures illustrating the different bird species are available from reception.

☑ Riding
☑ Pony trekking
☑ Crafts
☑ Diving
☑ Paintball
☑ Rafting
☑ Canyoning
☑ Aerial walkways
☑ Canoeing
☑ Hot-air ballooning

☑ Birdwatching
☑ Paragliding
☑ Fishing
☑ Road/off-road cycling
☑ Adventure park

Facilities: Toilet facilities in five blocks are of a high standard (with free hot showers). Two blocks are heated. Solar energy used. Washing machines and dryers. Motorcaravan services. Gas supplies. Fridge hire. Supermarket. Restaurant. Play area and children's zoo. Games hall. Trampolines. Organised activities in July/Aug including children's club, excursions and sporting activities. Mountain bike tours. Fishing. Live entertainment. Bicycle hire. Internet access and WiFi. Off site: Riding 3 km. Golf 5 km. Within walking distance of waterfront and town. Restaurants nearby.

Open: 1 April - 15 October.

Directions: From the town of Bled drive along south shore of lake to its western extremity (some 2 km) to the site.
GPS: 46.36155, 14.08075

Charges guide

Per unit incl. 2 persons and electricity	€ 20,50 - € 28,50
extra person	€ 8,50 - € 12,50
child (7-13 yrs)	€ 5,95 - € 8,75
dog	€ 1,50 - € 2,50

Camping Terme 3000

Kranjceva ulica 12, SLO-9226 Moravske Toplice
t: **025 121 200** e: **recepcija.camp2@terme3000.si**
alanrogers.com/SV4410 www.terme3000.si

Accommodation: ☑ Pitch ☐ Mobile home/chalet ☐ Hotel/B&B ☐ Apartment

Camping Terme 3000 is a large site with 430 pitches. There are 200 places for touring units (all with 16A electricity), the remaining pitches being taken by seasonal campers. On a grass and gravel surface (hard tent pegs may be needed), the level, numbered pitches are of 50-100 sq.m. There are hardstandings available in the newer area of the site. The site is part of an enormous thermal spa and fun pool complex (free entry to campers) under the same name. Here there are over 5,000 sq.m. of water activities – swimming, jet streams, waterfalls, water massages, four water slides (the longest is 170 m) and thermal baths. The complex also provides bars and restaurants and a large golf course. There are 14 indoor and outdoor pools, or you could go walking or cycling through the surrounding woods and fields, or try the delicious wines of the Goricko region.

Special offers
Access to the pool complex is free for campsite guests. There are 14 indoor and outdoor pools.

You might like to know
Visit the Freerider cycle centre for bicycle hire and details of guided trips.

- ☑ Riding
- ☑ Tennis
- ☑ Cycling *(road)*
- ☑ Sports field
- ☑ Outdoor pool
- ☑ Golf
- ☑ Paintball
- ☑ Hiking
- ☑ 10-pin bowling

Facilities: Modern and clean toilet facilities provide British style toilets, open washbasins and controllable, free hot showers. Laundry facilities. Football field. Tennis. Water gymnastics. Daily activity programme for children. Golf. WiFi (charged).

Open: All year.

Directions: From Maribor, go east to Murska Sobota. From there go north towards Martjanci and then east towards Moravske Toplice. Access to the site is on the right before the bridge. Then go through a park for a further 500 m.
GPS: 46.67888, 16.22165

Charges guide

Per unit incl. 2 persons and electricity	€ 36,50 - € 40,00
extra person	€ 16,00 - € 18,00
child (6-9 yrs)	€ 8,00 - € 9,00
child (10-14 yrs)	€ 11,20 - € 13,60
dog	€ 4,00

SLOVENIA – Catez ob Savi

Camping Terme Catez

Topliska cesta 35, SLO-8251 Catez ob Savi
t: 074 936 700 e: info@terme-catez.si
alanrogers.com/SV4415 www.terme-catez.si

Accommodation: ☑Pitch ☑Mobile home/chalet ☐ Hotel/B&B ☐ Apartment

Terme Catez is part of the modern Catez thermal spa, which includes very large and attractive indoor (31ºC) and outdoor swimming complexes, both with large slides and waves. The campsite has 450 pitches, with 190 places for tourers, arranged on one large, open field, with some young trees – a real sun trap – and provides level, grass pitches which are numbered by markings on the tarmac access roads. All have 10A electricity connections. Although the site is ideally placed for an overnight stop when travelling on the E70, it is well worthwhile planning to spend some time here to take advantage of the excellent facilities that are included in the overnight camping charges. The site is in the centre of a large complex which caters for most needs with its pools, large shopping centre, gym and the numerous events that are organised, such as the Magic School and Junior Olympic Games for children.

You might like to know
Winter and summer thermal aquapark with over 12,500 sq.m. of thermal water surface (indoor and outdoor swimming pools, water attractions, water park for children). Special preventative and rehabilitation programmes for sportsmen and women.

☑ Tennis
☑ Cycling (road)
☑ Sports field
☑ Outdoor pool
☑ Archery
☑ Golf
☑ Paintball
☑ Hiking
☑ Kayaking
☑ Fitness/gym

☑ Go-karting
☑ 10-pin bowling
☑ Fishing
☑ Sauna
☑ Squash

Facilities: Two modern toilet blocks with British style toilets, washbasins in cabins, large and controllable hot showers. Child sized basins. Facilities for disabled visitors. Dishwashing and laundry facilities. Motorcaravan service point. Supermarket. Kiosks for fruit, newspapers, souvenirs and tobacco. Attractive restaurant with buffet. Bar with terrace. Large indoor and outdoor swimming complexes. Rowing boats. Jogging track. Fishing. Golf. Bicycle hire. Sauna. Solarium. Riding. Organised activities. Video games. WiFi throughout (free). Off site: Golf 7 km.

Open: All year.

Directions: The site is signed from the Ljubljana-Zagreb motorway (E70) 6 km. west of the Slovenia/Croatia border, close to Brezice. GPS: 45.89137, 15.62598

Charges guide

Per unit incl. 2 persons and electricity	€ 39,50 - € 48,50
dog	€ 4,00
extra person	€ 17,50 - € 22,00
child (4-12 yrs)	€ 8,75 - € 11,00

SLOVENIA – Ptuj

Camping Terme Ptuj

Pot v toplice 9, SLO-2251 Ptuj
t: 027 494 100 e: info@terme-ptuj.si
alanrogers.com/SV4440 www.terme-ptuj.si

Accommodation: ☑Pitch ☑Mobile home/chalet ☐ Hotel/B&B ☐ Apartment

Camping Terme Ptuj is close to the river, just outside the interesting town of Ptuj. It is a small site with 100 level pitches, all for tourers and all with 10A electricity. In two areas, the pitches to the left are on part grass and part gravel hardstanding and are mainly used for motorcaravans. The pitches on the right hand side are on grass under mature trees, off a circular, gravel access road. The main attraction of this site is clearly the adjacent thermal spa and fun pool complex that also attracts many local visitors. It has several slides and fun pools, as well as a sauna, solarium and spa bath. The swimming pools and saunas are free for campsite guests. This site would also be a useful stopover en route to Croatia and the beautiful historic towns of Ptuj and Maribor are well worth a visit.

Facilities: Modern toilet block with British style toilets, open washbasins and controllable, hot showers (free). En-suite facilities for disabled visitors with toilet and basin. Two washing machines. Football field. Torch useful. Off site: Bar/restaurant and snack bar and large thermal spa 100 m.

Open: All year.

Directions: From Maribor go southeast towards Ptuj or exit the new (2009) A4 motorway at exit for Ptuj. Follow Golf/Therm signs, drive past spa/therm complex, camping is a further 100 m. GPS: 46.422683, 15.85495

Charges guide

Per person	€ 14,50 - € 16,50
child (6-10 yrs)	€ 7,25 - € 8,25
electricity	€ 4,00
dog	€ 4,00

You might like to know
The thermal park has no fewer than six swimming pools and the longest water slide in Slovenia!

- ☑ Riding
- ☑ Pony trekking
- ☑ Tennis
- ☑ Cycling *(road)*
- ☑ Cycling *(mountain biking)*
- ☑ Sports field
- ☑ Outdoor pool
- ☑ Crafts
- ☑ Sailing
- ☑ Windsurfing

- ☑ Golf
- ☑ Paintball
- ☑ Skiing *(downhill)*
- ☑ Kayaking
- ☑ Climbing wall

SLOVENIA – Verzej

Camping Terme Banovci

Banovci 1A, SLO-9241 Verzej
t: 251 314 00   e: terme@terme-banovci.si
alanrogers.com/SV4445   www.terme-banovci.si

Accommodation: ☑ Pitch ☑ Mobile home/chalet ☐ Hotel/B&B ☐ Apartment

Terme Banovci is a comfortable, quiet, countryside site with 130 normal touring pitches plus 50 FKK naturist pitches which are located separately. The grassed pitches have ample shade, are accessed by gravel roads and all have 10A electricity. Entry to the indoor (35-38°C) and outdoor (25-27°C) pools with a total surface area of 2,000 square metres is free to campers. The pools with large outdoor slide and ample space for sunbathing are all that one expects from a modern, well equipped, thermal spa. The comfortable restaurant is built in traditional style and drinks and food are available on the terrace beside the pool. The indoor pool contains mineral thermal water which is pumped up from a depth of 1,700 m. The water is rich in fluorides and recognised as being beneficial in treating rheumatism and other ailments. The outdoor pool is filled with normal water and is equipped with underwater massage jets, whirlpools, a waterfall and water slide. In addition there is a children's paddling pool.

You might like to know

Please note: this is partly a naturist campsite, the first in Europe to be developed around a thermal complex.

☑ Riding
☑ Tennis
☑ Cycling (road)
☑ Outdoor pool
☑ Crafts
☑ Archery
☑ Paintball
☑ Rafting
☑ Fishing

Facilities: Two well appointed heated sanitary blocks. Washbasins in cabins. Facilities for disabled visitors. Laundry. Motorcaravan service point. Nordic walking. Volleyball. Tennis. Morning gymnastics. Entertainment programme. Wellness centre with three Finnish saunas. Solarium. Turkish bath. Various massage programmes (at extra cost). Off site: Numerous walking and cycling paths

Open: 1 April - 6 November.

Directions: Site is 38 km. east of Maribor. From A5 take Vucja Vas exit and head south on the 230 for 5 km. to Knzevci pri Ljutomeru. Then turn northeast on the 439 for 1 km. and fork right to Banovci. Site is 400 m northeast of Banovci and is signed in the village.
GPS: 46.573181, 16.171494

Charges guide

Per unit incl. 2 persons and electricity	€ 27,50 - € 29,50
dog	€ 3,00

Balatontourist Camping Füred

Széchenyi út 24., H-8230 Balatonfüred (Veszprem County)
t: **87 580 241**　e: **fured@balatontourist.hu**
alanrogers.com/HU5090　www.balatontourist.hu

Accommodation:　☑ Pitch　☑ Mobile home/chalet　☐ Hotel/B&B　☐ Apartment

This is a large international holiday village rather than just a campsite. Pleasantly decorated with flowers and shrubs, it offers a very wide range of facilities and sporting activities. All that one could want for a family holiday can be found here. The 890 individual pitches (60-120 sq.m), all with electricity (6/10A), are on either side of hard access roads on which pitch numbers are painted. Many bungalows are for rent. Mature trees cover about two thirds of the site giving shade, with the remaining area being in the open. Directly on the lake with 800 m. of access for boats and bathing, there is a large, grassy area for relaxation, a small beach area for children and a variety of watersports. A water ski drag lift is most spectacular with its four towers erected in the lake to pull skiers around the circuit. There is a swimming pool on site with lifeguards. Along the main road that runs through the site are shops and kiosks, with the main bar/restaurant and terrace overlooking the lake.

You might like to know

Between early July and late August, the campsite offers activity programmes which repeat every second week, so there is always plenty to choose from.

- ☑ Riding
- ☑ Tennis
- ☑ Cycling *(road)*
- ☑ Outdoor pool
- ☑ Sailing
- ☑ Windsurfing
- ☑ Diving
- ☑ Waterskiing
- ☑ Fishing
- ☑ Free water slide

Facilities: Five fully equipped toilet blocks around the site include hot water for dishwashing and laundry (cleaning and maintenance variable). Private cabins for rent. Laundry service. Numerous bars, restaurants, cafés, food bars and supermarket (15/5-15/9). Stalls and kiosks with wide range of goods and souvenirs. Excellent swimming pool (1/6-31/8). Sandy beach. Large free water chute. Entertainment for children. Sports activities organised for adults. Sauna. Fishing. Water ski lift. Windsurf school. Sailing. Pedalos. Play area. Bicycle hire. Tennis. Minigolf. Video games. WiFi (charged). Dogs are not accepted. Off site: Close by, a street of fast food bars offers a variety of Hungarian and international dishes with attractive outdoor terraces under trees. Riding and golf 10 km.

Open: 27 April - 30 September.

Directions: Site is just south of Balatonfüred, at the traffic circle on Balatonfüred - Tihany road is well signed. Gates closed 13.00-15.00 except at weekends. GPS: 46.94565, 17.87709

Charges guide

Per unit incl. 2 persons and electricity	HUF 3600 - 9200
extra person	HUF 800 - 1600
child (2-14 yrs)	HUF 500 - 1200

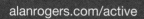

HUNGARY – Martfü

Martfü Health & Recreation Centre

Tüzép út, H-5435 Martfü (Jász-Nagkyun-Szolnok County)
t: **56 580 531** e: **martfu@camping.hu**
alanrogers.com/HU5255 www.martfu-turizmus.hu

Accommodation: ☑ **Pitch** ☑ **Mobile home/chalet** ☐ Hotel/B&B ☐ Apartment

The Martfü campsite is a modern site with 61 touring pitches on grassy terrain with rubber hardstandings. Each is around 90 sq.m. and separated by young bushes and trees. All have electricity (16/25A), waste water drainage, cable and satellite TV. There is a water tap per two pitches. There is no shade as yet, which may cause the site to become a real suntrap in summer, when temperatures may rise up to 34 degrees. A small lake and its beach on the site will cool you off. The main attraction at this site is the thermal spa, which is said to aid people with skin and rheumatic problems. Martfü is right on the banks of the River Tisza, which also makes it an excellent spot for those who enjoy watersports and fishing. The village of Martfü is close with numerous shops, restaurants and bars.

You might like to know
There is an excellent local spa and wellness centre.

- ☑ **Riding**
- ☑ **Pony trekking**
- ☑ **Tennis**
- ☑ **Cycling** *(road)*
- ☑ **Cycling** *(mountain biking)*
- ☑ **Sailing**
- ☑ **Golf**
- ☑ **Hiking**
- ☑ **Canoeing**
- ☑ **Fishing**

Facilities: Two modern, heated toilet blocks with British style toilets, open style washbasins, and free, controllable hot showers. Children's toilet and shower. Heated baby room. En-suite facilities for disabled visitors. Laundry. Kitchen with cooking rings. Motorcaravan services. Shop for basics. Takeaway for bread and drinks. Welcoming bar with satellite TV and WiFi. Indoor and outdoor swimming pools. Bowling. Library. Sauna. Jacuzzi. Playing field. Tennis. Minigolf. Fishing. Bicycle hire. Watersports. English is spoken. Off site: Fishing 50 m. Boat launching 1.5 km. Riding 5 km.

Open: All year.

Directions: Driving into Martfü from the north on the 442 road, take the first exit at the roundabout (site is signed). Continue for about 800 m. and site is signed on the right.
GPS: 47.019933, 20.268517

Charges guide

Per person	HUF 1200
child (6-14 yrs)	HUF 600
pitch	HUF 900 - 1200

No credit cards.

HUNGARY – Révfülöp

Balatontourist Camping Napfény

Halász u. 5, H-8253 Révfülöp (Veszprem County)
t: 87 563 031   e: napfeny@balatontourist.hu
alanrogers.com/HU5370   www.balatontourist.hu

Accommodation: ☑Pitch ☑Mobile home/chalet ☐ Hotel/B&B ☐ Apartment

Camping Napfény, an exceptionally good site, is designed for families with children of all ages looking for an active holiday, and has a 200 m. frontage on Lake Balaton. The site's 370 pitches vary in size (60-110 sq.m) and almost all have shade – very welcome during the hot Hungarian summers – and 6/10A electricity. As with most of the sites on Lake Balaton, a train line runs just outside the site boundary. There are steps to get into the lake and canoes, boats and pedalos for hire. An varied entertainment programme is designed for all ages and there are several bars and restaurants of various styles. There are souvenir shops and a supermarket. In fact, you need not leave the site at all during your holiday, although there are several excursions on offer, including to Budapest or to one of the many Hungarian spas, a trip over Lake Balaton or a traditional wine tour.

You might like to know
Camping Napfény is very child friendly with plenty of activities aimed at younger guests, including a new paddling pool.

☑ Cycling *(road)*
☑ **Sports field**
☑ **Windsurfing**
☑ **Kayaking**
☑ **Pedalos**
☑ **Fishing**
☑ **Free water slide**
☑ **Trampoline**
☑ **Beach volleyball**
☑ **Table tennis**

Facilities: The three excellent sanitary blocks have toilets, washbasins (open style and in cabins) with hot and cold water, spacious showers (both preset and controllable), child sized toilets and basins, and two bathrooms (hourly charge). Heated baby room. Facilities for disabled campers. Launderette. Dog shower. Motorcaravan services. Supermarket. Several bars, restaurants and souvenir shop. Children's pool. Sports field. Minigolf. Fishing. Bicycle hire. Canoe, rowing boats and pedalo hire. Extensive entertainment programme for all ages. Internet access (charged). Off site: Tennis 300 m. Riding 3 km.

Open: 30 April - 30 September.

Directions: Follow road 71 from Veszprém southeast to Keszthely. Site is in Révfülöp. GPS: 46.829469, 17.640164

Charges guide

Per unit incl. 2 persons and electricity	HUF 3400 - 7150
extra person	HUF 800 - 1200
child (2-14 yrs)	HUF 550 - 900
dog	HUF 550 - 900

AUSTRIA – Natters

Ferienparadies Natterer See

Natterer See 1, A-6161 Natters (Tirol)
t: 051 254 6732 e: info@natterersee.com
alanrogers.com/AU0060 www.natterersee.com

Accommodation: ☑ Pitch ☑ Mobile home/chalet ☐ Hotel/B&B ☐ Apartment

In a quiet location arranged around two lakes and set amid beautiful alpine scenery, this site founded in 1930 is renowned as one of Austria's top sites. Over the last few years many improvements have been carried out and pride of place goes to the innovative, award-winning multifunctional building at the entrance to the site. This contains all of the sanitary facilities expected of a top site, including a special children's section, private bathrooms to rent and also a dog bath. The reception, shop, café/bar/bistro and cinema are on the ground floor, and on the upper floor is a panorama lounge where the owner has assembled the largest collection of model camping cars and caravans in Europe. Almost all of the 235 pitches are for tourers. They are terraced, set on gravel/grass, all have electricity and most offer a splendid view of the mountains. The site's lakeside restaurant with bar and large terrace has a good menu and is the ideal place to spend the evening. There is a bus every hour and the city centre is only 19 minutes away.

You might like to know

The campsite is open all year around and is situated close to the city of Innsbruck, a former Winter Olympic Games city.

- ☑ Riding
- ☑ Tennis
- ☑ Cycling *(mountain biking)*
- ☑ Golf
- ☑ Skiing *(downhill)*
- ☑ Curling
- ☑ Ice skating
- ☑ Ice hockey
- ☑ Sail boats
- ☑ Paragliding

Facilities: The large, heated sanitary block has some private cabins, plus excellent facilities for babies, children and disabled visitors. Laundry facilities. Motorcaravan services. Fridge box hire. Bar. Restaurant and takeaway. Pizzeria. Good shop. Playgrounds. Children's activities. Day nursery in high season. Sports field. Archery. Games/TV room with Sky. Open-air cinema. Mountain bike hire. Aquapark (1/5-30/9). Surf bikes and pedalos. Canoes and mini sailboats for rent. Fishing. Entertainment programme (mid May-mid Oct). Dogs are not accepted in high season (July/Aug). WiFi (charged). Off site: Tennis and minigolf nearby. Riding 6 km. Golf 12 km.

Open: All year.

Directions: From Inntal autobahn (A12) take Brenner autobahn (A13) as far as Innsbruck-sud, Natters exit (no. 3). Turn left by Shell petrol station onto the B182 to Natters. At roundabout take first exit and immediately right again and follow signs to site 4 km. Do not use sat nav for final approach to site, follow camping signs. GPS: 47.23755, 11.34201

Charges guide

Per unit incl. 2 persons and electricity	€ 23,40 - € 34,60
extra person	€ 5,90 - € 8,30
child (under 13 yrs)	€ 4,60 - € 6,10

AUSTRIA – Kramsach

Camping Seehof

Reintalersee, Moosen 42, A-6233 Kramsach (Tirol)
t: 053 376 3541 e: info@camping-seehof.com
alanrogers.com/AU0065 www.camping-seehof.com

Accommodation: ☑ Pitch ☑ Mobile home/chalet ☐ Hotel/B&B ☐ Apartment

Camping Seehof is a family run site and excellent in every respect. It is situated in a marvellous, sunny and peaceful location on the eastern shores of Reintalersee lake. The site's comfortable restaurant has a terrace with lake and mountain views and serves local dishes as well as homemade cakes and ice cream. The site is in two areas: a small one next to the lake is ideal for sunbathing, the other larger one ajoins the excellent sanitary block. There are 170 pitches, 130 of which are for touring (20 tent pitches), are served by good access roads and have electricity (16A Europlug) and TV points; 80 pitches are fully serviced. Seehof provides an ideal starting point for walking, cycling or riding (with a riding stable nearby) and skiing in winter. The Alpbachtal Seeland card is available without cost at reception and allows free bus transport and free daily entry to many worthwhile attractions in the region. With easy access from the autobahn A12 the site is also a useful overnight stop. Bread is available from 07.00 each morning.

Special offers
Guests are issued with the Alpbachtal Card on arrival, which offers reductions on a wide range of local attractions.

You might like to know
Lots of exciting activities are available at the Kramsach outdoor centre, including skydiving, archery, whitewater swimming and canyoning.

☑ Riding
☑ Pony trekking
☑ Tennis
☑ Short tennis (half court)
☑ Cycling (road)
☑ Cycling (mountain biking)
☑ Sports field
☑ Outdoor pool
☑ Crafts
☑ Archery

☑ Golf
☑ Rafting
☑ Canyoning
☑ Potholing
☑ Rock climbing

Facilities: The sanitary facilities are first class and include ten bathrooms to rent for private use. Baby room. Facilities for disabled visitors. Dog shower. Washing machine and dryer. Ski room. Motorcaravan service point. Small shop. Good restaurant. Playground. WiFi throughout (charged). Bicycle hire. Fishing. Apartments to rent. Renovated Fitness and Play rooms. Off site: Tiroler farmhouse museum 1 km. Kramsach 3 km. Rottenberg 4 km. Swarovski Kristallwelten.

Open: All year.

Directions: From the A12 take Kramsach exit and follow the signs 'Zu den Seen' past Camping Krummsee and northern shore of lake, then right at the crossroads. Camping Seehof (300 m) is the first campsite you reach. Park on left, reception is on the right, follow campsite directions. GPS: 47.46188, 11.90734

Charges guide

Per unit incl. 2 persons and electricity	€ 17,30 - € 26,30
extra person	€ 4,60 - € 6,90
child (2-14 yrs)	€ 3,00 - € 4,50
dog	€ 3,00

Aktiv-Camping Prutz Tirol

Pontlatzstrasse 22, A-6522 Prutz (Tirol)
t: **054 722 648** e: **info@aktiv-camping.at**
alanrogers.com/AU0155 www.aktiv-camping.at

Accommodation: ☑ Pitch ☑ Mobile home/chalet ☐ Hotel/B&B ☐ Apartment

Aktiv-Camping is a long site which lies beside, and is fenced off from, the River Inn. Most of the 100, 80 sq. m, individual level pitches are for touring. They all have 6A electrical connections and in the larger area fit together sideways and back to back. Consequently, the site can sometimes have the appearance of being quite crowded. There is a separate overnight area for motorcaravans. This is an attractive area with many activities in both summer and winter for all age groups. You may consider using this site not just as an overnight stop, but also for a longer stay. From Roman times, when the Via Augusta passed through, this border region's stategic importance has left behind many fortifications that today feature among its many tourist attractions. Others include rambling, cycling and mountain biking, swimming in lakes and pools as well interesting, educational and adventurous activities for children. The Tiroler Summer card is available free at reception and has offers and discounts on many attractions.

You might like to know

Hikers will be rewarded with a wonderful view from the Kaunertaler glacier.

- ☑ **Riding**
- ☑ **Tennis**
- ☑ **Cycling** *(mountain biking)*
- ☑ **Outdoor pool**
- ☑ **Rock climbing**
- ☑ **Skiing** *(downhill)*
- ☑ **Snowboarding**
- ☑ **Pedaloes**
- ☑ **Fishing**
- ☑ **Nordic walking**

Facilities: The sanitary facilities are of a high standard, with private cabins and good facilities for disabled visitors. Baby room. Washing machine. Dog shower. Small shop (all year). Bar (15/5-15/9). Takeaway (15/5-15/9). Play room. Ski room. Skating rink. Children's entertainment. Guided walks, skiing (free shuttle service). WiFi throughout. Off site: Riding 1 km. Indoor pool at Feichten, Pilgrim's Church at Kaltenbrunn. Kaunertaler Glacier.

Open: All year.

Directions: Travelling west from Innsbruck on the E60/A12 for about 65 km. Exit at Landeck and follow the B315 (direction Reschenpass) turn south onto the B180 signed Bregenz, Arlberg, Innsbruck and Fernpass for 11 km. to Prutz. Site is signed to the right from the B180 over the bridge. GPS: 47.08833, 10.65831

Charges guide

Per unit incl. 2 persons and electricity	€ 16,00 - € 25,90
extra person	€ 4,00 - € 7,20
child (5-14 yrs)	€ 2,50 - € 4,00
dog	€ 2,50 - € 3,50

SWITZERLAND – Frutigen

Camping Grassi

Grassiweg 60, CH-3714 Frutigen (Bern)
t: 033 671 1149 e: campinggrassi@bluewin.ch
alanrogers.com/CH9360 www.camping-grassi.ch

Accommodation: ☑Pitch ☑Mobile home/chalet ☐ Hotel/B&B ☐ Apartment

This is a small site with about half the pitches occupied by static caravans, used by their owners for weekends and holidays. The 70 or so places available for tourists are not marked out but it is said that the site is not allowed to become overcrowded. Most places are on level grass with two small terraces at the end of the site. There is little shade but the site is set in a river valley with trees on the hills which enclose the area. Electricity is available for all pitches but long leads may be required in parts. It would make a useful overnight stop en-route for Kandersteg and the railway station where cars can join the train for transportation through the Lotschberg Tunnel to the Rhône Valley and Simplon Pass, or for a longer stay to explore the Bernese Oberland.

You might like to know
Some typically Tyrolean sports can be enjoyed at a nearby adventure park.

☑ Tennis
☑ Cycling (road)
☑ Cycling (mountain biking)
☑ Outdoor pool
☑ Crafts
☑ Rock climbing
☑ Hiking
☑ Skiing (downhill)
☑ Snowboarding
☑ Fishing

Facilities: The well constructed, heated sanitary block is of good quality. Washing machine and dryer. Gas supplies. Motorcaravan services. Communal room with TV. Kiosk (1/7-31/8). Play area and play house. Mountain bike hire. Fishing. Bicycle hire. WiFi. Off site: Shops and restaurants 10 minutes walk away in village. Riding 2 km. Outdoor and indoor pools, tennis and minigolf in Frutigen. A new sauna and wellness centre has recently opened in the village. Skiing and walking.

Open: All year.

Directions: Take Kandersteg road from Spiez and leave at Frutigen Dorf exit from where site is signed. GPS: 46.58173, 7.64219

Charges guide

Per unit incl. 2 persons and electricity	CHF 25,80 - 32,30
extra person	CHF 6,40
child (1-16 yrs)	CHF 1,50 - 3,20
dog	CHF 1,50

Camping Manor Farm 1

CH-3800 Interlaken-Thunersee (Bern)
t: 033 822 2264 e: manorfarm1@swisscamps.ch
alanrogers.com/CH9420 www.manorfarm.ch

Accommodation: ☑ Pitch ☑ Mobile home/chalet ☐ Hotel/B&B ☐ Apartment

Manor Farm has been popular with British visitors for many years, as this is one of the traditional touring areas of Switzerland. The flat terrain is divided into 525 individual, numbered pitches which vary considerably both in size (60-100 sq.m) and price. There is shade in some places. There are 144 pitches equipped with electricity (4/13A), water and drainage, and 55 also have cable TV connections. Reservations can be made, although you should find space, except perhaps in late July/early August when the best places may be taken. Around 40 per cent of the pitches are taken by permanent or letting units and a tour operator. The site lies outside the town on the northern side of the Thuner See, with most of the site between road and lake but with one part on the far side of the road. Interlaken is very much a tourist town, but the area is rich in scenery with innumerable mountain excursions and walks available. The lakes and Jungfrau railway are near at hand.

You might like to know
The campsite is located on the shores of Lake Thun amid beautiful mountain scenery and with numerous opportunities for watersports and excursions. Also open in winter.

☑ Riding
☑ Cycling (road)
☑ Outdoor pool
☑ Sailing
☑ Windsurfing
☑ Golf
☑ Hiking
☑ Fishing

Facilities: Seven separate toilet blocks are practical, heated and fully equipped, with free hot water for baths and showers. Twenty private toilet units are for rent. Laundry facilities. Motorcaravan services. Gas supplies. Excellent shop (1/4-15/10). Site-owned restaurant adjoining (1/3-30/10). Snack bar with takeaway (1/7-20/8). TV room. Playground and paddling pool. Minigolf. Bicycle hire. Sailing and windsurfing school. Lake swimming. Boat hire (slipway for your own). Fishing. Daily activity and entertainment programme in high season. Excursions. Max. 1 dog. WiFi (charged). Off site: Golf (18 holes) 500 m. (handicap card). Riding 3 km. Good area for cycling and walking.

Open: All year.

Directions: Site is 3 km. west of Interlaken. Follow signs for 'Camp 1'. From A8 (bypassing Interlaken) take exit 24 marked 'Gunten, Beatenberg', which is a spur road bringing you out close to site. GPS: 46.68129, 7.81524

Charges guide

Per unit incl. 2 persons and electricity	CHF 37,00 - 63,50
per person	CHF 10,50
child (6-15 yrs)	CHF 5,00
dog	CHF 4,00

SWITZERLAND – Interlaken

Camping Lazy Rancho 4

Lehnweg 6, CH-3800 Interlaken (Bern)
t: 033 822 8716 e: info@lazyrancho.ch
alanrogers.com/CH9430 www.lazyrancho.ch

Accommodation: ☑ Pitch ☑ Mobile home/chalet ☐ Hotel/B&B ☐ Apartment

This super site is in a quiet location with fantastic views of the dramatic mountains of Eiger, Monch and Jungfrau. Neat, orderly and well maintained, the site is situated in a wide valley just 1 km. from Lake Thun and 1.5 km. from Interlaken. The English speaking owners lovingly care for the site and will endeavour to make you feel very welcome. Connected by gravel roads, the 155 pitches, of which 90 are for touring units, are on well tended level grass (some with hardstanding, all with 10A electricity). 28 pitches also have water and waste water drainage. This is a quiet friendly site, popular with British visitors. The owners offer advice on day trips out, and how to get the best bargains which can be had on the railway.

You might like to know

The summit of the Niesen Mountain can be reached by funicular railway; from there you can enjoy the great views of Lake Thun and the Bernese Oberland.

- ☑ Riding
- ☑ Cycling (road)
- ☑ Cycling (mountain biking)
- ☑ Golf
- ☑ Rafting
- ☑ Canyoning
- ☑ Rock climbing
- ☑ Fishing
- ☑ Parachuting
- ☑ Paragliding

Facilities: Two good sanitary blocks are both heated with free hot showers, good facilities for disabled campers and a baby room. Laundry. Campers' kitchen with microwave, cooker, fridge and utensils. Motorcaravan service point. Well stocked shop. TV and games room. Play area. Small swimming pool. Bicycle hire (June-Aug). Free WiFi. Free bus in the Interlaken area – bus stop is five minutes walk from site. Off site: Cycle trails and way-marked footpaths. Riding 500 m. Golf and bicycle hire 1 km. Lake Thun for fishing 1.5 km. Boat launching 1.5 km. Interlaken (free regular bus service) and leisure centre 2 km.

Open: 1 May - 15 October.

Directions: Site is on north side of Lake Thun. From road 8 (Thun - Interlaken) on south side of lake take exit 24 Interlaken West. Follow towards lake at roundabout then follow signs for campings. Lazy Rancho is Camp 4. The last 500 m. is a little narrow but no problem. GPS: 46.68605, 7.830633

Charges guide

Per unit incl. 2 persons and electricity	CHF 26,50 - 47,70
extra person	CHF 6,00 - 6,60
child (6-15 yrs)	CHF 3,50 - 3,80
dog	CHF 3,00

alanrogers.com/active

47

Camping Jungfrau

CH-3822 Lauterbrunnen (Bern)
t: **033 856 2010** e: **info@camping-jungfrau.ch**
alanrogers.com/CH9460 www.camping-jungfrau.ch

Accommodation: ☑ Pitch ☑ Mobile home/chalet ☐ Hotel/B&B ☐ Apartment

This friendly site has a very imposing and dramatic situation in a steep valley with a fine view of the Jungfrau at the end. It is a popular site and, although you should usually find space, in season do not arrive too late. A fairly extensive area with grass pitches and hardcore access roads. All 391 pitches (250 for touring) have shade in parts, electrical connections (13A) and 50 have water and drainage also. Over 30% of the pitches are taken by seasonal caravans and it is used by two tour operators. Family owned and run by Herr and Frau Fuchs, you can be sure of a warm welcome and English is spoken. You can laze here amid real mountain scenery, though it does lose the sun a little early. There are many active pursuits available in the area, as well as trips on the Jungfrau railway and mountain lifts.

You might like to know
There is a ski store on site and a free bus to ski resorts in the winter season.

- ☑ **Cycling** (road)
- ☑ **Cycling** (mountain biking)
- ☑ **Sports field**
- ☑ **Rock climbing**
- ☑ **Hiking**
- ☑ **Skiing** (downhill)
- ☑ **Skiing** (cross-country)
- ☑ **Snowboarding**
- ☑ **Aerial walkways**
- ☑ **Ice skating**

Facilities: Three fully equipped modern sanitary blocks can be heated in winter and one provides facilities for disabled visitors. Baby baths. Laundry facilities. Motorcaravan services. Well equipped campers' kitchen. Excellent shop with photo printing facility. Self-service restaurant with takeaway (May-end Oct). General room with tables and chairs, TV, drink machines, amusements. Playgrounds and covered play area. Excursions and some entertainment in high season. Mountain bike hire. Internet point and WiFi. ATM. Drying room. Ski store. Off site: Free bus to ski station (in winter only).

Open: All year.

Directions: Go through Lauterbrunnen and fork right at far end (look for signpost) before road bends left, 100 m. before church. The final approach is not very wide.
GPS: 46.58807, 7.91077

Charges guide

Per person	CHF 9,80 - 11,90
child (6-15 yrs)	CHF 4,80 - 5,50
pitch incl. electricity (plus meter in winter)	CHF 17,00 - 29,50
dog	CHF 3,00

Camping Eienwäldli

Wasserfallstrasse 108, CH-6390 Engelberg (Unterwalden)
t: **041 637 1949** e: **info@eienwaeldli.ch**
alanrogers.com/CH9570 **www.eienwaeldli.ch**

Accommodation: ☑Pitch ☑Mobile home/chalet ☐ Hotel/B&B ☐ Apartment

This super site has facilities which must make it one of the best in Switzerland. It is in a beautiful location 3,500 feet above sea level, surrounded by mountains on the edge of the delightful village of Engelberg. Half of the site is taken up by static caravans, which are grouped together at one side. The camping area is in two parts; nearest the entrance there are 57 hardstandings for caravans and motorcaravans, all with electricity (metered) and beyond this is a flat meadow for about 70 tents. Reception can be found in the very modern foyer of the Eienwäldli Hotel which also houses the indoor pool, health complex, shop and café/bar.The indoor pool has been most imaginatively rebuilt as a Felsenbad spa bath with adventure pool, steam and relaxing grottoes, Kneipp's cure, children's pool with water slides, solarium, Finnish sauna and eucalyptus steam bath (charged). Being about 35 km. from Luzern by road and with a rail link, it makes a quiet, peaceful base from which to explore the Vierwaldstattersee region.

You might like to know
The wellness area extends over 1,000 sq. m. on three separate floors.

- ☑ **Cycling** (road)
- ☑ **Cycling** (mountain biking)
- ☑ **Sports field**
- ☑ **Rock climbing**
- ☑ **Hiking**
- ☑ **Skiing** (downhill)
- ☑ **Skiing** (cross-country)
- ☑ **Snowboarding**
- ☑ **Aerial walkways**

Facilities: The main toilet block, heated in cool weather, is situated at the rear of the hotel and has free hot water in washbasins (in cabins) and (charged) showers. A new modern toilet block has been added near the top end of the site. Washing machines and dryers. Shop. Café/bar. Small lounge. Indoor pool complex. Ski facilities including a drying room. Large play area with rafting pool fed by fresh water from the mountain stream. Torches useful. TV. WiFi. Golf. Off site: Golf driving range and 18-hole course nearby. Fishing and bicycle hire 1 km. Riding 2 km.

Open: All year.

Directions: From N2 Gotthard motorway, leave at exit 33 Stans-Sud and follow signs to Engelberg. Turn right at T-junction on edge of town and follow signs to 'Wasserfall' and site. GPS: 46.80940, 8.42367

Charges guide

Per person	CHF 6,00 - 9,00
child (6-15 yrs)	CHF 3,00 - 4,50
pitch incl. electricity (plus meter)	CHF 10,00 - 17,00
dog	CHF 1,30 - 2,00

FRANCE – Orpierre

Camping des Princes d'Orange

F-05700 Orpierre (Hautes-Alpes)
t: 04 92 66 22 53   e: campingorpierre@wanadoo.fr
alanrogers.com/FR05000   www.campingorpierre.com

Accommodation: ☑Pitch ☑Mobile home/chalet ☐ Hotel/B&B ☐ Apartment

This attractive, terraced site, set on a hillside above the village has been thoughtfully developed. Muriel, the owner, speaks excellent English and the genuine, friendly welcome means many families return year upon year, bringing in turn new generations. Divided into five terraces, each with its own toilet block, some of its 100 generously sized pitches (96 for touring) enjoy good shade from trees and have electricity connections (10A). In high season, one terrace is reserved as a one-star camping area for young people. Orpierre also has an enchanting maze of medieval streets and houses, almost like a trip back through the centuries. Whether you choose to drive, climb, walk or cycle, there is plenty of wonderful scenery to discover in the immediate vicinity, whilst not far away, some exhilarating hang-gliding and parascending can be enjoyed. It is renowned as a world class rock climbing venue, with over 600 climbing routes in the surrounding mountains.

Special offers
In July and August, there are free guided hikes twice weekly and free mountain biking once a week (bikes can be hired)

You might like to know
The medieval village of Orpierre is surrounded by towering cliffs with over 500 possible climbs at all levels.

☑ Riding
☑ Pony trekking
☑ Cycling (road)
☑ Cycling (mountain biking)
☑ Outdoor pool
☑ Rafting
☑ Canyoning
☑ Rock climbing
☑ Aerial walkways
☑ Fishing

Facilities: Six well equipped toilet blocks. Baby bath. Laundry facilities. Bread. Bar (1/4-31/10). Heated swimming pool, paddling pool (15/6-15/9). Play area with inflatable climbing tower. Boules. Games room. Fridge hire. Only gas barbecues are permitted. Free WiFi around reception area. Off site: Orpierre with a few shops and bicycle hire 500 m. Fishing 7 km. Nearest shopping centre Laragne 12 km. Riding 19 km. Hang-gliding. Parascending. Rock climbing. Walking. Mountain biking. Gorges de Guil.

Open: 1 April - 31 October.

Directions: Turn off N75 road at Eyguians onto D30 - site is signed on left at crossroads in the centre of Orpierre village.
GPS: 44.31121, 5.69677

Charges guide

Per unit incl. 2 persons and electricity	€ 21,10 - € 27,70
extra person	€ 5,50 - € 7,80
child (under 7 yrs)	€ 3,00 - € 3,70
dog	€ 1,70

No credit cards.

Camping Green Park

159 Vallon des Vaux, F-06800 Cagnes-sur-Mer (Alpes-Maritimes)
t: 04 42 20 47 25 e: info@homair.com
alanrogers.com/FR06120 www.homair.com

Accommodation: ☑ Pitch ☑ Mobile home/chalet ☐ Hotel/B&B ☐ Apartment

Green Park is now part of the Homair group and currently managed by Max and Alex L'Honen. The part of the site which used to be on the opposite side of the road is now a campsite in its own right and also owned by Homair. Situated just over 4 km. from the beaches at Cagnes-sur-Mer, this is predominantly a site with many chalets and mobile homes for rent. There are just three pitches which are suitable for motorcaravans or caravans, the remaining 58 pitches are for tents only due to the steep incline on which the terraces are situated. In fact, after the second terrace, no children under ten years are allowed. Cars cannot be parked on the pitches but can park close by. The site has a lovely pool complex with restaurant and bar overlooking it as does the outdoor entertainment area. All facilities are open from the beginning of the season and carry on almost to the close. If you wish to venture further to visit the many attractions in the area or the beach, there is a bus stop outside the gate and a timetable in reception.

You might like to know

Guests at Green Park are also permitted to use the excellent amenities at Camping le Todos, which is adjacent.

- ☑ Tennis
- ☑ Cycling *(road)*
- ☑ Sports field
- ☑ Outdoor pool
- ☑ Crafts
- ☑ Sailing
- ☑ Diving
- ☑ Waterskiing
- ☑ Pedaloes

Facilities: All the toilets are modern and mostly British style, with facilities for children and disabled visitors (the disabled facilities are superb). Showers and washbasins are modern and kept very clean. Dishwashing and laundry sinks and three washing machines. Bar, restaurant and takeaway. Two swimming pools. Internet point. WiFi (charged). Games room. Electronic barrier (€5 card deposit) and a gate keeper on duty all night. Off site: Beach 4 km. Golf and riding 9 km.

Open: 2 April - 2 October.

Directions: From Aix, A8, exit 47 onto N7 towards Nice. Straight on at traffic lights, by racecourse, for 2 km. Turn left towards Val Fleuri, avenue du Val Fleuri. Over roundabouts to Chemin Vallon des Vaux, site on right 2 km. Avoid the town centre. GPS: 43.68901, 7.15598

Charges guide

Per unit incl. 2 persons and electricity	€ 24,00 - € 44,00
small tent with electricity	€ 16,00 - € 29,00
extra person	€ 4,50 - € 7,50
child (3-6 yrs)	€ 3,00 - € 5,50

FRANCE – Villeneuve-de-Berg

Domaine le Pommier

RN102, F-07170 Villeneuve-de-Berg (Ardèche)
t: 04 75 94 82 81 e: info@campinglepommier.com
alanrogers.com/FR07110 www.campinglepommier.com

Accommodation: ☑ Pitch ☑ Mobile home/chalet ☐ Hotel/B&B ☐ Apartment

Domaine Le Pommier is an extremely spacious, Dutch owned site of ten hectares in 32 hectares of wooded grounds centred around a spectacular pirate themed water park. The site is steeply terraced and has wonderful views over the Ardèche mountains and beyond. There are 611 pitches, with 275 for touring units, the rest used for mobile homes and chalets for rent. They are on sandy grass, of a good size and well spaced. Separated by trees and hedges, some have less shade. All have access to electricity and water is close by. The site is not recommended for very large units. Extensive amenities feature a mini-farm, including llamas, goats and ponies. The site has first class facilities. These include the most up-to-date toilet blocks, a very good bar/restaurant and one of the best pirate themed swimming and paddling pool complexes we have seen with amazing water slides with varying levels of thrill and excitement – ideal for all the family. The poolside catering is good and this area could keep you occupied all day.

You might like to know

The site is just 1,500 m. (at an altitude of 300 m!) from the village of Villeneuve-de-Berg with its 2,500 inhabitants. The village was founded in 1284 and became famous for the cultivation of mulberry trees for silk production.

- ☑ Cycling *(mountain biking)*
- ☑ Sports field
- ☑ Archery
- ☑ Canyoning
- ☑ Potholing
- ☑ Rock climbing
- ☑ Hiking
- ☑ Canoeing
- ☑ Water games
- ☑ Orienteering

Facilities: Four excellent toilet blocks, one with underfloor heating, provide all the necessary facilities. Comprehensive shop. Bar/restaurant. Swimming pool complex with exciting slides, paddling pools, etc. Everything opens all season. Boules. Minigolf. Large multisports area. Activities including games in the woods, archery, water polo and tug-of-war. Bridge and water colour classes. Tennis. Soundproofed disco. Very extensive programme of events on and off site. Low season excursions. Entertainment programme exclusively in Dutch. WiFi (charged). Off site: Villeneuve-de-Berg 1.5 km. River Ardèche 12 km. Potholing, rock climbing, canoeing, canyoning, mountain biking, walking and riding.

Open: 21 April - 15 September.

Directions: Site is west of Montélimar on the N102. The entrance is adjacent to the roundabout at the eastern end of the Villeneuve-de-Berg bypass. GPS: 44.57250, 4.51115

Charges guide

Per unit incl. 2 persons and electricity	€ 23,50 - € 43,50
extra person	€ 5,50 - € 9,50
child (4-12 yrs)	€ 3,50 - € 6,50
dog	free - € 4,50

FRANCE – La Bastide-de-Sérou

Camping l'Arize

Lieu-dit Bourtol, F-09240 La Bastide-de-Sérou (Ariège)
t: **05 61 65 81 51** e: **camparize@aol.com**
alanrogers.com/FR09020 www.camping-arize.com

Accommodation: ☑ Pitch ☑ Mobile home/chalet ☐ Hotel/B&B ☐ Apartment

The site sits in a delightful, tranquil valley among the foothills of the Pyrenees and is just east of the interesting village of La Bastide-de-Sérou beside the River Arize (good trout fishing). The river is fenced for the safety of children on the site, but may be accessed just outside the gate. The 70 large pitches are neatly laid out on level grass within the spacious site. All have 3/6A electricity and are separated into bays by hedges and young trees. An extension to the site gives 24 large, fully serviced pitches (10A) and a small toilet block. You will receive a warm welcome from Dominique and Brigitte at this friendly little family site, and Brigitte speaks excellent English. Discounts have been negotiated for several of the local attractions (details are provided in the comprehensive pack provided on arrival – in your own language). This is a comfortable and relaxing base for touring this beautiful part of the Pyrenees with easy access to the medieval town of Foix and even Andorra for duty-free shopping.

Special offers
Special golf discounts and special rates for canyoning are available.

You might like to know
There are over 100 km. of waymarked trails within easy reach of the site.

- ☑ Riding
- ☑ Pony trekking
- ☑ Tennis
- ☑ Cycling (road)
- ☑ Cycling (mountain biking)
- ☑ Outdoor pool
- ☑ Golf
- ☑ Paintball
- ☑ Rafting
- ☑ Hiking
- ☑ Kayaking
- ☑ Fitness/gym
- ☑ 10-pin bowling
- ☑ Fishing

Facilities: Toilet block includes facilities for babies and disabled visitors. Laundry room. Motorcaravan services. New shop and restaurant planned. Small swimming pool and sunbathing area. Entertainment in high season. Weekly barbecues and welcome drinks on Sundays. Fishing, riding and bicycle hire. WiFi.
Off site: Several restaurants and shops within a few minutes drive. The nearest restaurant is located at the national stud for the famous Merens horses just 200 m. away and will deliver takeaway meals to your pitch. Golf 5 km.

Open: 12 March - 10 November.

Directions: Site is southeast of the village La Bastide-de-Sérou. Take the D15 towards Nescus and site is on right after about 1 km. GPS: 43.00182, 1.44538

Charges guide

Per unit incl. 2 persons and electricity	€ 16,40 - € 28,30
extra person	€ 4,20 - € 5,80
child (2-12 yrs)	€ 2,80 - € 4,90
dog	€ 1,20 - € 2,20

FRANCE – Le Trein d'Ustou

Camping le Montagnou

Route de Guzet, F-09140 Le Trein d'Ustou (Ariège)
t: 05 61 66 94 97   e: campinglemontagnou@wanadoo.fr
alanrogers.com/FR09030   www.lemontagnou.com

Accommodation: ☑ Pitch ☑ Mobile home/chalet ☐ Hotel/B&B ☐ Apartment

The road going south out of St Girons appears to lead to nowhere other than Guzet, but it is a 30 km. detour over fairly easy roads to the little village of Le Trein d'Ustou. Just before Le Trein d'Ustou you will find Le Montagnou, a small, friendly, English run campsite nestling among the lush lower slopes of the mountains. Richard and Nicola welcome you to this quiet base for touring this lovely area, or for taking part in the many activities available locally. Ther are 40 level pitches on grass for tourers and tents, all with electricity (6/10A), plus two large luxury safari tents and two mobile homes for hire. At a lower level, there is an area of the river running alongside the site which the locals use for swimming. Other activities in the area are walking, mountain biking, geocaching, nature trails, fishing, horse riding, caves, underground rivers, thermal springs and a summer spa.

You might like to know
The area offers a vast range of nature, cultural and heritage activities. We are 10 km. from the small village of Seix, which has a supermarket, a baker, a butcher and restaurants.

- ☑ Riding
- ☑ Cycling *(road)*
- ☑ Cycling *(mountain biking)*
- ☑ Outdoor pool
- ☑ Rafting
- ☑ Rock climbing
- ☑ Hiking
- ☑ Aerial walkways
- ☑ Kayaking
- ☑ Fishing
- ☑ Canyoning
- ☑ Paragliding
- ☑ Geocaching
- ☑ Luge

Facilities: Two toilet blocks can be heated and include washbasins in cabins, covered dishwashing and laundry sinks, washing machine and dryers, and good facilities for disabled visitors. Snack bar with takeaway. Gas supplies. Baker delivers (July/August). Library (English and French books). Fishing. Family room (board games). Boules. Table tennis. WiFi. Children's play area. Off site: Restaurant 50 m. in the village. Shops at Seix. Riding 15 km. Spa. Nature trails. Mountain biking. Caves.

Open: 1 March - 30 September.

Directions: From the A64 take D117 to St Girons. Take the D618 south towards Oust and Guzet and 3 km. north of Guzet turn right onto D3 passing Oust and Seix. At Pont de la Taule turn left on D8 for 7 km. to Trein d'Ustou. Site is on left before village. GPS: 42.811238, 1.255381

Charges guide

Per unit incl. 2 persons and electricity	€ 16,50 - € 21,70
extra person	€ 4,50
child (under7 yrs)	€ 2,80
dog	€ 2,00

No credit cards.

FRANCE – Locunolé

Castel Camping le Ty-Nadan

Route d'Arzano, F-29310 Locunolé (Finistère)
t: 02 98 71 75 47   e: infos@camping-ty-nadan.fr
alanrogers.com/FR29010   www.camping-ty-nadan.fr

Accommodation: ☑Pitch ☑Mobile home/chalet ☐ Hotel/B&B ☐ Apartment

Camping le Ty-Nadan is a well organised site set amongst wooded countryside along the bank of the River Elle. There are 183 grassy pitches for touring units, many with shade and 99 fully serviced. The pool complex with slides and paddling pool is very popular as are the large indoor pool complex and indoor games area with a climbing wall. There is also an adventure play park and a Minikids park for 5-8 year olds, not to mention tennis courts, table tennis, pool tables, archery and trampolines. This is a wonderful site for families with children. Several tour operators use the site.
An exciting and varied programme of activities is offered throughout the season – canoeing and sea kayaking expeditions, rock climbing, mountain biking, aquagym, paintball, horse riding or walking – all supervised by qualified staff. A full programme of entertainment for all ages is provided in high season including concerts, Breton evenings with pig roasts, dancing, etc. (be warned, you will be actively encouraged to join in)!

You might like to know
All the on-site activities are led by fully qualified staff. There are plenty of opportunities too for fishing, cycling and mountain biking.

- ☑ Riding
- ☑ Pony trekking
- ☑ Tennis
- ☑ Archery
- ☑ Paintball
- ☑ Rock climbing
- ☑ Zip wires
- ☑ Canoeing
- ☑ Kayaking
- ☑ Climbing wall

- ☑ Adventure park
- ☑ Quad bikes

Facilities: Two older, split-level toilet blocks are of fair quality and include washbasins in cabins and baby rooms. A newer block provides easier access for disabled campers. Washing machines and dryers. Restaurant, takeaway, bar and well stocked shop. Heated outdoor pool (17x8 m). Indoor pool. Small river beach (unfenced). Indoor badminton and rock climbing facility. Activity and entertainment programmes (all season). Horse riding centre. Bicycle hire. Boat hire. Canoe trips. Fishing. Internet access and WiFi (charged). Off site: Beaches 20 minutes by car. Golf 12 km.

Open: 27 March - 2 September.

Directions: Make for Arzano which is northeast of Quimperlé on the Pontivy road and turn off D22 just west of village at site sign. Site is about 3 km. GPS: 47.90468, -3.47477

Charges guide

Per unit incl. 2 persons and electricity	€ 20,10 - € 46,00
extra person	€ 4,30 - € 8,80
child (2-6 yrs)	€ 2,00 - € 5,40
dog	€ 2,10 - € 5,80

FRANCE – Hourtin-Plage

Airotel Camping la Côte d'Argent

F-33990 Hourtin-Plage (Gironde)
t: 05 56 09 10 25 e: info@cca33.com
alanrogers.com/FR33110 www.cca33.com

Accommodation: ☑ Pitch ☑ Mobile home/chalet ☑ Hotel/B&B ☐ Apartment

Côte d'Argent is a large, well equipped site for leisurely family holidays. It makes an ideal base for walkers and cyclists with over 100 km. of cycle lanes in the area. Hourtin-Plage is a pleasant invigorating resort on the Atlantic coast and a popular location for watersports enthusiasts. The site's top attraction is its pool complex, where wooden bridges connect the pools and islands and there are sunbathing and play areas plus an indoor heated pool. The site has 588 touring pitches (all with 10A electricity), not always clearly defined, arranged under trees with some on sand. High quality entertainment takes place at the impressive bar/restaurant near the entrance. Spread over 20 hectares of undulating sand-based terrain and in the midst of a pine forest. The site is well organised and ideal for children.

Special offers
Free activities in July/August: children's club (6-11 yrs), evening entertainment, sporting and other activities.

You might like to know
There is plenty to occupy visitors to site – the large aquatic complex (3500 m²) with covered, heated pool, a multisports court and the Activity Centre with shops, games room, bicycle hire, video games and fitness room.

☑ Riding
☑ Pony trekking
☑ Tennis
☑ Crafts
☑ Archery
☑ Waterskiing
☑ Aerial walkways
☑ Kayaking
☑ Pedaloes
☑ Fishing

☑ Play area
☑ Sailing
☑ Surfing
☑ Canoeing
☑ Boating

Facilities: Very clean sanitary blocks include provision for disabled visitors. Washing machines. Motorcaravan service points. Large supermarket, restaurant, takeaway, pizzeria, bar (all open 1/6-15/9). Four outdoor pools with slides and flumes (1/6-19/9). Indoor pool (all season). Fitness room. Massage (Institut de Beauté). Play areas. Miniclub, organised entertainment in season. Tennis. Bicycle hire. WiFi (charged). ATM. Charcoal barbecues are not permitted. Hotel (12 rooms). Off site: Path to the beach 300 m. Fishing and riding. Golf 30 km.

Open: 14 May - 18 September.

Directions: Turn off D101 Hourtin-Soulac road 3 km. north of Hourtin. Then join D101E signed Hourtin-Plage. Site is 300 m. from the beach. GPS: 45.22297, -1.16465

Charges guide

Per unit incl. 2 persons and electricity	€ 26,00 - € 48,00
extra person	€ 4,00 - € 8,00
child (3-9 yrs)	€ 3,00 - € 7,00
dog	€ 2,00 - € 6,00

Camping le Tedey

Par le Moutchic, route de Longarisse, F-33680 Lacanau-Lac (Gironde)
t: 05 56 03 00 15   e: camping@le-tedey.com
alanrogers.com/FR33290   www.le-tedey.com

Accommodation: ☑ Pitch ☑ Mobile home/chalet   ☐ Hotel/B&B   ☐ Apartment

With direct access to a large lake and beach, this site enjoys a beautiful tranquil position set in an area of 14 hectares amidst mature pine trees. There are 700 pitches of which 630 are for touring units, with just 38 mobile homes and chalets available for rent. The pitches are generally level and grassy although parts of the site are on a slope. The pitches are shady with dappled sunlight breaking through the trees. Electricity is available to all pitches and 223 also have water and waste water drainage. The bar is close to the lake with a large indoor and outdoor seating area. There is an open-air cinema on Saturdays and Wednesdays as well as other entertainment in July and August. A children's club is also organised. The takeaway sells a variety of food and the shop next door is well stocked. This is an attractive, well maintained site where you get a feeling of space and calm. There are many places of interest nearby and it is a short drive from Bordeaux. The friendly owners and staff are helpful and English is spoken.

You might like to know
Why not visit the bustling city of Bordeaux? It's less than one hour away.

☑ Riding

☑ Cycling (road)

☑ Cycling (mountain biking)

☑ Sailing

☑ Windsurfing

☑ Golf

☑ Hiking

☑ Canoeing

☑ Pedaloes

☑ Fishing

Facilities: Four modern sanitary blocks with facilities for disabled visitors and babies. Laundry facilities. Shop. Bar with terrace (1/6-15/9). Crêperie (16/6-11/9). Takeaway (25/6-3/9). Bicycle hire. Boating on the lake. Fishing. Pétanque. Playground. Gas barbecues only on pitches. Dogs are not accepted in July/Aug. WiFi (charged). Off site: Surfing. Riding. Golf. Cycling.

Open: 28 April - 19 September.

Directions: From Lacanau take the D6 to Lacanau-Océan. Take Route de Longarisse and the site is well signed. GPS: 44.98620, -1.13410

Charges guide

Per unit incl. 2 persons and electricity	€ 21,00 - € 26,00

FRANCE – Pierrefitte-sur-Sauldre

Leading Camping les Alicourts

Domaine des Alicourts, F-41300 Pierrefitte-sur-Sauldre (Loir-et-Cher)
t: 02 54 88 63 34 e: info@lesalicourts.com
alanrogers.com/FR41030 www.lesalicourts.com

Accommodation: ☑ Pitch ☑ Mobile home/chalet ☐ Hotel/B&B ☐ Apartment

A secluded holiday village set in the heart of the forest, with many sporting facilities and a super spa centre, Parc des Alicourts is midway between Orléans and Bourges, to the east of the A71. There are 490 pitches, 150 for touring and the remainder occupied by mobile homes and chalets. All pitches have electricity connections (6A) and good provision for water, and most are 150 sq.m. (min. 100 sq.m). Locations vary, from wooded to more open areas, thus giving a choice of amount of shade. All facilities are open all season and the leisure amenities are exceptional. The Senseo Balnéo centre offers indoor pools, hydrotherapy, massage and spa treatments for over 18s only (some special family sessions are provided). An inviting outdoor water complex (all season) includes two swimming pools, a pool with wave machine and a beach area, not forgetting three water slides. Competitions and activities are organised for adults and children including a high season club for children with an entertainer twice a day.

Special offers
Family activity passes are available and there are numerous free activities.

You might like to know
All activities are available from the day the site opens to the day it closes.

☑ Pony trekking
☑ Tennis
☑ Cycling (road)
☑ Sports field
☑ Outdoor pool
☑ Archery
☑ Golf
☑ Canoeing
☑ Kayaking
☑ Pedaloes

☑ Fitness/gym
☑ Go-karting
☑ Fishing
☑ Mini-disc golf
☑ Minigolf

Facilities: Three modern sanitary blocks include some washbasins in cabins and baby bathrooms. Laundry facilities. Facilities for disabled visitors. Motorcaravan services. Shop. Restaurant. Takeaway in bar with terrace. Pool complex. Spa centre. 7-hectare lake (fishing, bathing, canoes, pedaloes). 9-hole golf course. Adventure play area. Tennis. Minigolf. Boules. Roller skating/skateboarding (bring own equipment). Bicycle hire. Internet access and WiFi (charged).

Open: 29 April - 9 September.

Directions: From A71, take Lamotte Beuvron exit (no 3) or from N20 Orléans to Vierzon turn left on to D923 towards Aubigny. After 14 km. turn right at camping sign on to D24E. Site signed in 4 km. GPS: 47.54398, 2.19193

Charges guide

Per unit incl. 2 persons and electricity	€ 20,00 - € 44,00
extra person	€ 7,00 - € 10,00
child (5-17 yrs)	€ 6,00 - € 8,00
child (1-4yrs)	free - € 6,00
dog	€ 5,00 - € 7,00

FRANCE – Brissac

Camping de l'Etang

Route de Saint-Mathurin, F-49320 Brissac (Maine-et-Loire)
t: 02 41 91 70 61   e: info@campingetang.com
alanrogers.com/FR49040   www.campingetang.com

Accommodation: ☑ Pitch ☑ Mobile home/chalet   ☐ Hotel/B&B   ☐ Apartment

At Camping de l'Etang many of the 124 level touring pitches have pleasant views across the countryside. Separated and numbered, some have a little shade and all have electricity with water and drainage nearby. 21 are fully serviced. A small bridge crosses the river Aubance which runs through the site (well fenced) and there are two lakes where fisherman can enjoy free fishing. The site has its own vineyard and the wine produced can be purchased on the campsite. The adjacent Parc de Loisirs is a paradise for young children with many activities (free for campers). These include boating, pedaloes, pony rides, miniature train, water slide, bouncy castle and swings. Originally the farm of the Château de Brissac (yet only 24 km. from the lovely town of Angers), this is an attractive campsite retaining much of its rural charm. A Sites et Paysages member.

Special offers

One free admission per person to the amusement park with stays of 1 to 3 nights; 10 free admissions per family for stays over 3 nights. Once these are used, campers are admitted at a reduced rate

You might like to know

In association with local clubs, we can offer canoeing trips on the Loire, with the possibility of a night-time outing each week. Campsite visitors enjoy preferential rates.

☑ Riding
☑ Pony trekking
☑ Cycling (road)
☑ Sports field
☑ Outdoor pool
☑ Crafts
☑ Golf
☑ Aerial walkways
☑ Zip wires
☑ Canoeing

☑ Pedaloes
☑ Climbing wall
☑ Hot-air ballooning
☑ Fishing

Facilities: Three well maintained toilet blocks provide all the usual facilities. Laundry facilities. Baby room. Disabled visitors are well catered for. Motorcaravan service point. The farmhouse houses reception, small shop and takeaway snacks (July/Aug) when bar is closed.
A bar/restaurant serves crêpes, salads, etc. (evenings July/Aug). Swimming pool (heated and covered) and paddling pool. Fishing. Play area. Bicycle hire. Wide variety of evening entertainment in high season. WiFi. No electric barbecues. Off site: Golf and riding 10 km. Sailing 25 km.

Open: 15 May - 15 September.

Directions: Brissac-Quincé is 17 km. southeast of Angers on D748 towards Poitiers. Do not enter the town but turn north on D55 (site signed) in direction of St Mathurin.
GPS: 47.3611, -0.4353

Charges guide

Per unit incl. 2 persons and electricity	€ 18,00 - € 30,00
extra person	€ 4,00 - € 5,00
child (3-10 yrs)	€ 2,00 - € 3,00
dog	€ 2,00 - € 4,00

FRANCE – Agos-Vidalos

Camping Soleil du Pibeste

16 avenue du Lavedan, F-65400 Agos-Vidalos (Hautes-Pyrénées)
t: **05 62 97 53 23** e: **info@campingpibeste.com**
alanrogers.com/FR65090 www.campingpibeste.com

Accommodation: ☑Pitch ☑Mobile home/chalet ☐ Hotel/B&B ☐ Apartment

The Dusserm family, owners, are very proud of their regional culture and heritage and will ensure you are a made welcome. The reception is friendly, with an area for local foods, maps and good tourist information. This site is special because of the range and type of activities that it offers. These include tai chi, qi gong, massage, archery, walking, climbing and canoeing. Choral and creative activities are offered. There are 38 touring pitches all with 3-15A electricity. Mobile homes and chalets are available to rent. The mountain view from the terrace is magnificent. Ongoing improvements include a second swimming pool incorporating facilities for campers with disabilities. Play areas are being expanded to cater for different age groups, including lively teenagers. There is a shop and bread can be ordered for delivery the following morning. The bar and restaurant area is large and well equipped. The site is rural but has a bus stop just outside providing access to Argeles-Gazost and the renowned pilgrimage town of Lourdes.

Special offers
Inclusive packages with accommodation rental and activities – you can put together your own daily programme. Safety is always the top priority with activities run by fully-qualified instructors.

You might like to know
A variety of courses are on offer, with qualified instructors.

- ☑ Riding
- ☑ Pony trekking
- ☑ Tennis
- ☑ Outdoor pool
- ☑ Crafts
- ☑ Archery
- ☑ Paintball
- ☑ Rafting
- ☑ Canyoning
- ☑ Potholing
- ☑ Rock climbing
- ☑ Hiking
- ☑ Skiing *(downhill)*
- ☑ Aerial walkways
- ☑ Zip wires

Facilities: Two heated toilet blocks. Baby room. Facilities for disabled visitors (key). Cleaning can be variable. Washing machine, dryer. Motorcaravan services. Bar, snack bar, restaurant and pizzeria (June-Sept). Shop for essentials. Bread to order. Swimming pool with panoramic views and loungers (June-Sept). New children's play areas (4-6 yrs and 6-10 yrs). Multisports pitch. Volleyball. Tennis. Badminton. Bowling. Basketball. 4 free activities weekly (tai chi, qi gong, rollerblading, archery, etc; July/Aug). Entertainment programme, children's activities and craft workshops (July/Aug). Massage (charged). Library. WiFi (charged). Off site: Fishing 800 m. Rafting 2 km. Golf 10 km. Riding 15 km. Skiing 20 km.

Open: 1 May - 30 September.

Directions: Agos Vidalos is on the N21, which becomes the D821, 5 km. south of Lourdes. Leave express-way at second exit, signed Agos Vidalos and continue on D921B to site, a short distance on the right. GPS: 43.03557, -0.07093

Charges guide

Per unit incl. 2 persons and electricity	€ 25,00 - € 34,00
extra person	€ 8,00
dog	€ 5,00

Homair La Palmeraie

Boulevard de la Plage, F-66440 Torreilles-Plage (Pyrénées-Orientales)
t: 04 68 28 20 64   e: campinglapalmeraie@homair.com
alanrogers.com/FR66160   www.homair.com

Accommodation: ☑ Pitch ☑ Mobile home/chalet   ☐ Hotel/B&B   ☐ Apartment

La Palmeraie, now owned by Homair, is a family campsite situated some 900 metres from the beach at Torreilles-Plage. There is an abundance of foliage, including a variety of trees and flowering shrubs which provide ample shade – unusual in a situation on the littoral and so close to the sea. There are some 300 pitches in total, most of which are occupied by mobile homes or bengali tents. Some are privately owned and 180 are available to rent, leaving just 40 pitches for touring units. An attractive pool and surrounding sunbathing area, overlooked by the bar and restaurant, form the focal part of the site. Entertainment in the evening and sports activities during the day are organised in July and August, when there is also a club for children. There are plenty of activities in the local area including a beach club, sailing, karting and micro-flying. Perpignan is 12 km. and the border with Spain only 50 km.

You might like to know
Some of the activities you will enjoy include donkey rides, introductory microlight flights, children's jet ski circuit, minigolf, paintball and quad bikes.

☑ Riding
☑ Tennis
☑ Cycling *(road)*
☑ Cycling *(mountain biking)*
☑ Sports field
☑ Outdoor pool
☑ Sailing
☑ Windsurfing
☑ Kitesurfing
☑ Waterskiing

☑ Paintball
☑ Go-karting
☑ Fishing

Facilities: Sanitary blocks are traditional in style with modern fittings. Facilities for disabled visitors and children. Laundry facilities. Fridge hire. Shop. Bar, restaurant and takeaway (all open when site open). Swimming and paddling pools. Excellent large play area. Games room. Multisport court. Evening entertainment and organised sports activities in July/Aug. Children's club (6-12 yrs). WiFi throughout site. Off site: Bus stop outside entrance. Beach 900 m. Sailing, beach club, minigolf and other activities in the local area. Riding and fishing 2 km. Bicycle hire 5 km.

Open: 4 May - 18 September.

Directions: From A9 take exit 41 and follow signs for Canet via D81 and D83. Once on D83 look for signs for Torreilles-Plage. Site is on right hand side as you approach from the roundabout on the D83. GPS: 42.7657, 3.02740

Charges guide

Per unit incl. 2 persons and electricity (10A)	€ 15,00 - € 38,00
extra person	€ 4,00 - € 8,50
child (3-7 yrs)	€ 3,00 - € 4,50
dog	€ 5,00

No credit cards.

FRANCE – Sainte Marie-la-Mer

Camping le Lamparo

Route de la Plage, F-66470 Sainte Marie-la-mer (Pyrénées-Orientales)
t: **04 68 73 83 87** e: **info@campinglamparo.com**
alanrogers.com/FR66450 **www.campinglamparo.com/**

Accommodation: ☑Pitch ☑Mobile home/chalet ☐ Hotel/B&B ☐ Apartment

A small, family run site of just 156 pitches, Le Lamparo is hidden away on the edge of Sainte Marie-le-Mer. M. and Mme. Fischer, the owners, offer a very warm welcome and the environment for a good family holiday without all the noise and distractions that can often be found on larger sites. Large flat pitches provide ample space and there are differing degrees of shade and screening to suit most preferences. There is plenty to do on site and no need to drive out every day in search of activities or you can take advantage of the close proximity to both Sainte Marie town and the beach. There is a selection of accommodation to rent on site ranging from two person caravans to mobile homes for up to six people. There are also 'bungalows' which are a very strong vinyl reinforced square tent on a concrete base for four people.

You might like to know
There is plenty of activity in the swimming pool, including a regular aqua gym.

☑ **Tennis**
☑ **Cycling** *(road)*
☑ **Outdoor pool**
☑ **Crafts**
☑ **Windsurfing**
☑ **Waterskiing**
☑ **Golf**
☑ **Hiking**
☑ **Fitness/gym**
☑ **Fishing**

Facilities: Two toilet blocks are a good provision and a re bright with an open design. Some washbasins ion cabins. Dedicated facilities for babies and disabled people. Washing machines. Basic provisions from the bar (shops nearby). Bar and restaurant with takeaway. Good sized swimming pool. Jacuzzi, sauna and gym. Indoor games area. Outdoor sports facilities. Small play area. Activities for young children in high season. Off site: Resort facilities within 1.2 km. as well as the small town of Sainte-Marie. Riding, fishing, watersports and amusement parks all within 10 minutes drive.

Open: All year.

Directions: Leave A9 at exit 41 and take D83 towards St Laurent. Turn right on D81 and head south towards Sainte-Marie and site is signed at the roundabout. GPS: 42.72841, 3.02477

Charges guide

Per unit incl. 2 persons and electricity	€ 12,00 - € 27,00
extra person	€ 3,00 - € 7,00
child (under 4 yrs)	free - € 2,00
dog	€ 2,00 - € 4,00

62

FRANCE – Argelès-sur-Mer

Camping la Sirène

Route de Taxo á la Mer, F-66702 Argelès-sur-Mer (Pyrénées-Orientales)
t: 04 68 81 04 61   e: contact@camping-lasirene.fr
alanrogers.com/FR66560   www.camping-lasirene.fr

Accommodation: ☑ Pitch ☑ Mobile home/chalet   ☐ Hotel/B&B   ☐ Apartment

From the moment you step into the hotel-like reception area you realise that this large site offers the holiday maker everything they could want in a well managed and convenient location close to Argelès-sur-Mer and the beaches. The 740 mobile homes and chalets vary in standard but all are less than five years old, very clean, comfortable and located on neat tidy pitches. There are also some touring pitches. In the summer there are 170 staff on duty to ensure your stay is as enjoyable as they can make it. All the shops and amenities are near reception making the accommodation areas quite peaceful and relaxing. There are many things to do and summer visitors have the option of using the free bus service to the beach where the site has its own club where you can even go windsurfing at no charge.

You might like to know

There is a PADI and CMAS certified diving centre here. Beginners and experienced divers are both welcome at this excellent centre.

- ☑ Riding
- ☑ Pony trekking
- ☑ Tennis
- ☑ Cycling *(road)*
- ☑ Cycling *(mountain biking)*
- ☑ Sports field
- ☑ Outdoor pool
- ☑ Crafts
- ☑ Archery
- ☑ Sailing
- ☑ Windsurfing
- ☑ Diving
- ☑ Paintball
- ☑ Canyoning
- ☑ Hiking

Facilities: Restaurant, bar and takeaway. Large shop (all season). Large aqua park, paddling pools, slides, jacuzzi. Games room. Multisports field, tennis, archery, minigolf, football. Theatre, evening entertainment, discos, show time spectacular. Riding. Bicycle hire. Off site: Argelès-sur-Mer with beaches, karting, 10-pin bowling, amusement park and the site's private Emeraude Beach Club, all 2 km. Interesting old town of Collioure close by. Fishing 4 km. Golf 7 km.

Open: 17 April - 26 September.

Directions: Leave A9 motorway, junction 42, take D114, towards Argelès. Leave D114, junction 10 and follow signs for Plage Nord. Site signed after first roundabout. Site on right 2 km. after last roundabout. GPS: 42.57093, 3.02906

Charges guide

Per unit incl. 1-3 persons and electricity	€ 26,00 - € 43,00
extra person	€ 6,00 - € 9,00
child (under 5 yrs)	€ 4,00 - € 6,00
dog	free

FRANCE – Peisey-Nancroix

Camping les Lanchettes

F-73210 Peisey-Nancroix (Savoie)
t: **04 79 07 93 07** e: **lanchettes@free.fr**
alanrogers.com/FR73030 www.camping-lanchettes.com

Accommodation: ☑Pitch ☑Mobile home/chalet ☑Hotel/B&B ☐ Apartment

This site is close to the beautiful Vanoise National Park and at 1,470 m. is one of the highest campsites in this guide. There is a steep climb to the site but the spectacular scenery is well worth the effort. It is a natural, terraced site with 90 good size, reasonably level and well drained, grassy/stony pitches, with 70 used for touring units, all having electricity (3-10A). Outside taps are only available in summer because of the altitude and cold winters. For those who love walking and biking, wonderful scenery, flora and fauna, this is the site for you. Underpowered units are not advised to attempt the climb. In winter it is ideal for the serious skier being close to the famous resort of Les Arcs (via free bus service and cable car) and about 30 of the pitches at the bottom of the site are unused as they become part of a cross country ski run. A wide range of footpaths and mountain bike rides are available in the valley and mountains around. Some chair lifts carry bikes up to the walking/bike tracks; the descent is breathtaking.

Special offers
In summer, explore the mountains on a free guided ramble.

You might like to know
In summer, the ski lifts can be used to transport your mountain bike. All you have to do is enjoy the thrill of the descent, as you would in winter on skis.

- ☑ Riding
- ☑ Pony trekking
- ☑ Cycling *(mountain biking)*
- ☑ Golf
- ☑ Rafting
- ☑ Canyoning
- ☑ Rock climbing
- ☑ Aerial walkways
- ☑ Zip wires
- ☑ Fishing

- ☑ Rollerblading
- ☑ Paragliding
- ☑ Via Ferrata
- ☑ Adventure park
- ☑ Skiing/Winter sports

Facilities: Well appointed heated toilet block. Motorcaravan services. Restaurant, takeaway (July/Aug. and winter). Playground. Club/TV room. Large tent/marquee used in bad weather. In winter a small bus (free) runs to the ski lifts every 30 minutes. Free WiFi. Off site: Riding next to site. Peisey-Nancroix, restaurants, bars and shops 3 km. Les Arcs winter sports centre, outdoor swimming pool and bicycle hire 6 km. Golf and indoor pool 8 km. Lakeside beach 10 km. Walks in National Park.

Open: 15 December - 30 April,
1 June - 15 October.

Directions: From Albertville take N90 towards Bourg-St-Maurice, through Aime. In 9 km. turn right on D87, signed Peisey-Nancroix. Follow winding hilly road (with hairpin bends) for 10 km. Pass through Peisey-Nancroix; site on right about 1 km. beyond Nancroix.
GPS: 45.53137, 6.77560

Charges guide

Per unit incl. 2 persons and electricity	€ 12,50 - € 14,10
extra person	€ 4,20 - € 4,70
child (2-7 yrs)	€ 2,30 - € 2,55
dog	€ 1,30 - € 1,60

Camping le Parc Isertan

F-73710 Pralognan-la-Vanoise (Savoie)
t: 04 79 08 75 24 e: camping@camping-isertan.com
alanrogers.com/FR73200 www.camping-isertan.com

Accommodation: ☑ Pitch ☑ Mobile home/chalet ☐ Hotel/B&B ☐ Apartment

Le Parc Isertan is open for both summer and winter seasons and can be found at the heart of the Vanoise national park. It is located on the scenic GR55 long distance footpath. There are 180 pitches here, most of which have electrical connections, and many with fine views of the surrounding mountains, including La Grande Casse (3855 m). The pitches are mostly grassy and flat. The restaurant, 'La Fondue', which specialises in local cuisine, has a typically Savoyard style and is the focal point for the site. The bar is a good place to enjoy a vin chaud after a day exploring the mountains. A number of wooden chalets are available for rent, and a small hotel is located within the site. Pralognan is an important resort and is a good centre for trying various activity sports, such as parascending, glacier walking and via ferrata. A good range of winter sports can be experienced in the area. Other, rather more traditional activities are also on offer in the village, including tennis, riding and mountain biking.

You might like to know

Equipment hire and professional tuition for the various activities are available in the village of Pralognan la Vanoise, which has a wide range of amenities including shops, restaurants, a cinema and a weekly market.

- ☑ Riding
- ☑ Pony trekking
- ☑ Tennis
- ☑ Cycling *(road)*
- ☑ Cycling *(mountain biking)*
- ☑ Sports field
- ☑ Outdoor pool
- ☑ Crafts
- ☑ Rock climbing
- ☑ Hiking
- ☑ Skiing *(downhill)*
- ☑ Skiing *(cross-country)*
- ☑ Snowboarding
- ☑ Aerial walkways
- ☑ Zip wires

Facilities: Bar/restaurant. Small shop. Games room. TV room. Ski shuttle in winter. Children's play area. Tourist information. Chalets for rent. Off site: Swimming pool. Tennis. Pralognan centre. Walking and cycle tracks. Riding.

Open: 29 May - 24 September, 18 December - 18 April.

Directions: Approaching from the west, leave N90 at Moutiers and head south on D915 towards Courchevel, and continue to Pralognan (do not drive to Courchevel). The site is well indicated in the village. GPS: 45.37642, 6.7226

Charges guide

Per unit incl. 2 persons and electricity	€ 14,00 - € 31,50
extra person	€ 3,50 - € 7,20
child (acc. to age)	free - € 4,50
dog	free - € 1,50

FRANCE – Le Grand-Bornand

Camping Caravaning l'Escale

Route de la Patinoire, F-74450 Le Grand-Bornand (Haute-Savoie)
t: 04 50 02 20 69 e: contact@campinglescale.com
alanrogers.com/FR74070 www.campinglescale.com

Accommodation: ☑Pitch ☑Mobile home/chalet ☐ Hotel/B&B ☑ Apartment

You are assured a good welcome in English from the Baur family at this beautifully maintained and picturesque site, situated at the foot of the Aravis mountain range. There are 149 pitches with 122 for touring. Of average size, part grass, part gravel they are separated by trees and shrubs that give a little shade. All pitches have electricity (2-10A) and 86 are fully serviced. Rock pegs are essential. A 200-year-old building houses a bar/restaurant decorated in traditional style and offering regional dishes in a delightful, warm ambience. The village is 200 m. and has all the facilities of a resort with activities for both summer and winter holidays. In summer, a variety of well signed footpaths and cycle tracks provide forest or mountain excursions. In winter the area provides superb facilities for downhill- and cross-country skiing. This very popular campsite, set beside the picture postcard ski resort of Le Grand-Bornand, has wonderful views and is surrounded by fields of flowers in summer.

Special offers

For special offers on rental accommodation, please see the site's website: www.campinglescale.com. Short stays and one-night rentals are offered outside school holiday periods.

You might like to know

The campsite is open all year round, with rental of mobile homes, apartments, studios and rooms available throughout the year. In summer, a 240 sq.m. pool (80 sq.m. covered) with balnéo massaging jets is open.

- ☑ Pony trekking
- ☑ Tennis
- ☑ Cycling *(mountain biking)*
- ☑ Outdoor pool
- ☑ Archery
- ☑ Golf
- ☑ Rock climbing
- ☑ Hiking
- ☑ Skiing *(downhill)*
- ☑ Skiing *(cross-country)*
- ☑ Snowboarding
- ☑ Aerial walkways
- ☑ Zip wires
- ☑ Fishing
- ☑ Indoor/outdoor pools

Facilities: Good toilet blocks (heated in winter) have all the necessary facilities. Drying room. Superb pool complex (all season) and outdoor pools and paddling pools (15/6-29/8), jacuzzi and water jets. Cosy bar/restaurant and takeaway (all season). Play area. Tennis. WiFi. Activities for adults and children. Video games. Discounts on organised walks and visits to Chamonix-Mont Blanc. Off site: Village (5 minutes walk), shops, bars, restaurants, archery, paragliding, golf, minigolf. 150 km. of signed walks. Activities organised for children and adults. Ice skating, snow shoes in winter. Bicycle hire 200 m. Riding and golf 3 km. Free bus for cable car (500 m) for skiing and snowboarding.

Open: 15 December - 25 April, 1 June - 25 September.

Directions: From Annecy follow D16 and D909 towards La Clusaz. At St Jean-de-Sixt, turn left at roundabout D4 signed Grand-Bornand. Just before village fork right signed Vallée de Bouchet and camping. Site entrance is on right at roundabout in 1.2 km. GPS: 45.94036, 6.42842

Charges guide

Per unit incl. 2 persons and electricity	€ 20,30 - € 34,40
extra person (over 2 yrs)	€ 5,00 - € 5,90

FRANCE – Saint Gervais-les-Bains

Camping les Dômes de Miage

197 route des Contamines, F-74170 Saint Gervais-les-Bains (Haute-Savoie)
t: 04 50 93 45 96   e: info@camping-mont-blanc.com
alanrogers.com/FR74140   www.camping-mont-blanc.com

Accommodation: ☑Pitch ☑Mobile home/chalet   ☐ Hotel/B&B   ☐ Apartment

Saint Gervais is a pretty spa town in the picturesque Val-Monjoie valley and this site is 2 km. from its centre. It is 22 km. west of Chamonix and ideally located for discovering this marvellous mountain region. Nestled among the mountains, this sheltered, well equipped site provides 150 flat grassy pitches. Of a good size, about half have shade and there are 100 with electricity points (3-10A). The remainder on terraced ground are used for tents. Third generation hosts, Stéphane and Sophie, will welcome you to the site, and their passion for this area at the foot of Mont Blanc is infectious. A number of Savoyard style chalets to let are planned for the future. This is a good site for large motorcaravans. There is no on-site entertainment programme, but lots of information about the area and activities available nearby is provided at reception where they will help you plan your itinerary. There is a bus service into Saint Gervais, from where there is a frequent shuttle bus to its spa and a tramway to the Mont Blanc range.

Facilities: Two sanitary blocks, one heated, with a suite for disabled visitors and baby room. Washing machines, dryer. Motorcaravan services. Small basic shop. Bar/restaurant. TV room, library, ironing board. Excellent playground. Playing field. WiFi (free). Off site: Fishing 100 m. Bicycle hire 1 km. Riding 7 km. Shops, etc. and outdoor swimming pool in St Gervais.

Open: 1 May - 12 September.

Directions: From St Gervais take D902 towards Les Contamines and site is on left after 2 km. GPS: 45.87389, 6.7199

Charges guide

Per unit incl. 2 persons and electricity	€ 20,10 - € 26,10
extra person	€ 3,00 - € 4,10
child (2-9 yrs)	€ 2,50 - € 3,50
dog	free - € 2,00

You might like to know

There are plenty of activities on offer locally: indoor and outdoor pools, golf, fishing, fitness, rafting and canyoning, hiking, hot-air ballooning, go-karting, summer sledging, helicopter and plane flights, all within 25 km.

☑ Riding
☑ Pony trekking
☑ Tennis
☑ Short tennis *(half court)*
☑ Cycling *(road)*
☑ Cycling *(mountain biking)*
☑ Outdoor pool
☑ Archery
☑ Paintball
☑ Rafting

☑ Canyoning
☑ Rock climbing
☑ Hiking
☑ Skiing *(downhill)*
☑ Skiing *(cross-country)*

FRANCE – Doussard

Campéole la Nublière

30 allée de la Nublière, F-74210 Doussard (Haute-Savoie)
t: **04 50 44 33 44** e: **nubliere@wanadoo.fr**
alanrogers.com/FR74190 www.campeole.co.uk

Accommodation: ☑Pitch ☑Mobile home/chalet ☐ Hotel/B&B ☐ Apartment

If you are looking for large pitches, shady trees, mountain views and direct access to a lakeside beach, this site is for you. There are 271 touring pitches, of which 243 have electrical hook-ups (6A). This area is very popular and the site is very likely to be busy in high season. There may be some noise from the road and the public beach. La Nublière is 16 km. from old Annecy and you are spoilt for choice in how to get there. Take a ferry trip, hire a sailing boat or pedalo, or walk or cycle along the traffic free track towards the town. The local beach and sailing club are close and there is a good restaurant on the site perimeter. Across the road from the site are courts for tennis and boules. The site is perfect for walking, cycling or sailing and in low season provides a tranquil base for those just wishing to relax in natural surroundings on the edge of a nature reserve.

You might like to know

Annecy's old town is built along the banks of waterways running from the lake and is a delightful mixture of old and new, with colourful houses and chic boutiques.

- ☑ Riding
- ☑ Tennis
- ☑ Golf
- ☑ Rafting
- ☑ Canyoning
- ☑ Canoeing
- ☑ Kayaking
- ☑ Hot air ballooning
- ☑ Fishing
- ☑ Paragliding

Facilities: Large clean sanitary blocks include free hot showers and good facilities for disabled visitors. Laundry. Shop (1/5-15/9). Restaurant on site perimeter (closed Mon). Children's club (3/7-26/8) for 4-8 yrs. Safe deposit. WiFi (charged). Off site: Small supermarket adjacent to site. Good watersports area within 70 m. Access to town beach from site. Fishing 100 m. Golf and riding 4 km. Bicycle hire 7 km.

Open: 28 April - 18 September.

Directions: Site is 16 km. south of Annecy on Route d'Albertville, well signed.
GPS: 45.7908, 6.2197

Charges guide

Per unit incl. 2 persons and electricity	€ 17,50 - € 26,60
extra person	€ 4,50 - € 6,80
child (2-6 yrs)	free - € 4,30

FRANCE – Saint Aygulf

Camping Résidence du Campeur

B.P. 12, D7, F-83371 Saint Aygulf (Var)
t: **04 94 81 01 59** e: **info@residence-campeur.com**
alanrogers.com/FR83050 www.residence-campeur.com

Accommodation: ☑ Pitch ☑ Mobile home/chalet ☐ Hotel/B&B ☐ Apartment

This excellent site near the Côte d'Azur will take you away from all the bustle of the Mediterranean coast. Spread out over ten hectares, there are separate areas for mobile homes and touring caravans and tents, with pitches arranged along avenues. The 67 touring pitches average 100 sq.m. in size and all have electricity connections and private sanitary facilities (although washbasins double as dishwashing sinks). The bar/restaurant is surrounded by a shady terrace, whilst friendly staff provide an excellent service. A pleasant pool complex is available for those who wish to stay on site instead of going swimming in the nearby lake or from the Mediterranean beaches. Activities are organised daily during the summer season and the site has its own open-air cinema.

You might like to know
This region is well known for its fine sandy beaches, and one of the best is just 2.5 km. from this site.

- ☑ Riding
- ☑ Tennis
- ☑ Cycling *(road)*
- ☑ Sports field
- ☑ Outdoor pool
- ☑ Archery
- ☑ Golf
- ☑ Fishing
- ☑ Pétanque
- ☑ Minigolf

Facilities: Private toilet blocks are cleaned at regular intervals and include a washbasin, shower and WC. Laundry area with washing machines. Well stocked supermarket. Bar/restaurant. Takeaway (all open all season). New swimming pool complex with four water slides (high season). Two tennis courts. Minigolf. Boules. Fishing. Bicycle hire. Play area. Games/TV room. Only gas or electric barbecues are permitted. Off site: Riding 1.5 km. Golf 2 km. Beach and St Aygulf 2.5 km. Waterskiing nearby.

Open: 27 March - 30 September.

Directions: Leave A8 at Le Muy exit (no. 36) on N555 towards Draguignan then onto the N7 towards Fréjus. Turn right on D7 signed St Aygulf and site is on the right about 2.5 km. before the town. GPS: 43.40905, 6.70893

Charges guide

Per unit incl. 3 persons and electricity	€ 30,10 - € 50,15
extra person	€ 5,19 - € 8,65
child (under 7 yrs)	€ 3,54 - € 5,90
dog	€ 4,00

FRANCE – Roquebrune-sur-Argens

Camping les Pêcheurs

F-83520 Roquebrune-sur-Argens (Var)
t: 04 94 45 71 25 e: info@camping-les-pecheurs.com
alanrogers.com/FR83200 www.camping-les-pecheurs.com

Accommodation: ☑ Pitch ☑ Mobile home/chalet ☐ Hotel/B&B ☐ Apartment

Les Pêcheurs will appeal to families who appreciate natural surroundings together with many activities, cultural and sporting. Interspersed with mobile homes, the 150 good sized touring pitches (6/10A electricity) are separated by trees or flowering bushes. The Provençal style buildings are delightful, especially the bar, restaurant and games room, with its terrace down to the river and the site's own canoe station (locked gate). Across the road is a lake used exclusively for waterskiing with a sandy beach and restaurant. Enlarged spa facilities include a swimming pool, a large jacuzzi, massage, a steam pool and a sauna. Developed over three generations by the Simoncini family, this peaceful, friendly site is set in more than four hectares of mature, well shaded countryside at the foot of the Roquebrune Rock. Activities include climbing the 'Rock' with a guide. We were intrigued with stories about the Rock, and the Holy Hole, the Three Crosses and the Hermit all call for further exploration, which reception staff are happy to arrange.

You might like to know

There is a diving school on site, so what better opportunity to learn?

- ☑ Riding
- ☑ Cycling *(road)*
- ☑ Sports field
- ☑ Outdoor pool
- ☑ Diving
- ☑ Waterskiing
- ☑ Golf
- ☑ Rafting
- ☑ Canoeing
- ☑ Fishing

Facilities: Modern, refurbished, well designed toilet blocks, baby baths, facilities for disabled visitors. Washing machines. Shop. Bar and restaurant (all open all season). Heated outdoor swimming pool (all season), separate paddling pool (lifeguard in high season), ice cream bar. Games room. Spa facilities. Playing field. Fishing. Canoeing. Waterskiing. Rafting and diving schools. Activities for children and adults (high season), visits to local wine caves. Only gas or electric barbecues. WiFi in reception, bar/restaurant and pool area. Off site: Bicycle hire 1 km. Riding and golf 5 km. (reduced fees).

Open: 1 April - 30 September.

Directions: From A8 take Le Muy exit, follow N7 towards Fréjus for 13 km. bypassing Le Muy. After crossing A8, turn right at roundabout towards Roquebrune-sur-Argens. Site is on left after 1 km. just before bridge over river. GPS: 43.450783, 6.6335

Charges guide

Per unit incl. 2 persons and electricity	€ 23,00 - € 43,00
extra person	€ 4,00 - € 7,80
child (5-10 yrs)	€ 3,20 - € 6,20
dog (max. 1)	€ 3,20

FRANCE – Saint Julien-des-Landes

Castel Camping la Garangeoire

F-85150 Saint Julien-des-Landes (Vendée)
t: 02 51 46 65 39 e: info@garangeoire.com
alanrogers.com/FR85040 www.camping-la-garangeoire.com

Accommodation: ☑Pitch ☑Mobile home/chalet ☐ Hotel/B&B ☐ Apartment

La Garangeoire is a stunning campsite, situated some 15 km. inland near the village of St Julien-des-Landes. Set in 200 hectares of parkland surrounding the small château of La Garangeoire, of which there is an outstanding view as you approach through the gates. With a spacious, relaxed atmosphere, the main camping areas are on either side of the old road which is edged with mature trees. The 356 pitches, all named rather than numbered, are individually hedged, some with shade. They are well spaced and are especially large (most 150-200 sq.m), most with electricity (16A) and some with water and drainage also. Access is good for large units. Tour operators use 168 pitches. The parkland provides peaceful fields and woods for walking, and four lakes available for fishing, with boating on the main lake (lifejackets are provided). The site is now run by the third generation of owners since 1964, Ann and Eric Bourgon.

Facilities: Ample, first class sanitary facilities. All have washbasins in cabins. Facilities for babies and disabled guests. Laundry facilities. Motorcaravan service point. Shop, full restaurant and takeaway (10/5-22/9) with bars and terrace (all season). Pool complex with a new covered pool, water slides, fountains and a children's pool (all season). Play field with play equipment. Football pitch. Games room. Tennis courts. Multisports court. Bicycle hire. Minigolf. Archery. Riding (July/Aug). Fishing and boating. Bouncy castle. Trampolines. Quadricycles (on payment). Off site: Nature trails around the Lac de Jaunay 2 km. Golf 8 km. Sailing and surfing in Brétignolles-sur-Mer 12 km. Beaches 15 km.

Open: 7 April - 24 September.

Directions: Site is signed from St Julien; the entrance is to the east off the D21 road, 2.5 km. north of St Julien-des-Landes.
GPS: 46.66387, -1.71346

Charges guide

Per unit incl. 2 persons and electricity	€ 17,50 - € 37,00
extra person	€ 4,50 - € 7,90
child (under 10 yrs)	€ 2,50 - € 4,30
dog	€ 3,00 - € 4,00

Special offers
Free fishing in the estate's four lakes (from 3 to 8.5 acres).

You might like to know
On site are four signposted trails, a riding centre with qualified instructors, four fishing lakes, soccer school (high season) and a pedal-karting circuit.

- ☑ Riding
- ☑ Pony trekking
- ☑ Tennis
- ☑ Cycling (mountain biking)
- ☑ Outdoor pool
- ☑ Archery
- ☑ Canoeing
- ☑ Pedaloes
- ☑ Go-karting
- ☑ Fishing

- ☑ Covered pool

Camping Domaine de la Forêt

Route de Martinet, F-85150 Saint Julien-des-Landes (Vendée)
t: 02 51 46 62 11   e: camping@domainelaforet.com
alanrogers.com/FR85820 www.domainelaforet.com

Accommodation: ☑ Pitch ☑ Mobile home/chalet ☐ Hotel/B&B ☐ Apartment

Set in the tranquil and beautiful natural parkland surrounding an 18th-century château, this lovely site has 200 large pitches, of which 167 are for touring units. All are on grass and fully serviced including 6A electricity; some are in shady woodland and others, for sun worshippers, are more open. The camping area is only a small part of the 50-hectare estate, with a mix of woodland, open meadows and fishing lakes, all accessible to campers. The many outbuildings around the courtyard have been tastefully converted and include a bar and restaurant in the old stables. There are two outdoor swimming pools, one on each side of the château. Many sports, activities and entertainment are on offer, which should keep everyone satisfied. Children will have a great time here exploring the vast, unrestricted area and sometimes hidden corners of this site in Swallows and Amazons style. However, parents should note there are open, unfenced fishing lakes and barns with tractors and machinery.

You might like to know
Why not visit Le Puy du Fou? The evening spectacle is world class and highly recommended. During the day, the Grand Parc with its wildlife park, its floral park and entertainment is also a trip well worth making.

- ☑ Riding
- ☑ Tennis
- ☑ Sports field
- ☑ Outdoor pool
- ☑ Sailing
- ☑ Golf
- ☑ Canoeing
- ☑ Go-karting
- ☑ Fishing
- ☑ Quad bikes

Facilities: Two large good quality sanitary blocks include washbasins in cubicles, with good provision for babies and disabled campers. Laundry facilities with washing machines and dryers. Bar/restaurant with TV. Two heated outdoor swimming pools (one for children with slide, one for serious swimmers). Regular evening entertainment, children's clubs and disco (July/Aug). Adventure playground, trampoline and games room. Tennis. Boules. Fishing lakes. 6-hole swing golf course (pitch and putt with soft balls) and minigolf. Canoeing trips. WiFi. Only gas barbecues permitted. Off site: Equestrian centre, bicycle hire 200 m. La Mothe-Achard 5 km. Golf and beaches 12 km.

Open: 15 May - 15 September.

Directions: St Julien-des-Landes is 25 km. west of la Roche-sur-Yon, northwest of la Mothe-Achard. From la Mothe-Achard take D12 to St Julien, turn northeast on D55 at crossroads towards Martinet. Site is almost immediately on left (signed). GPS: 46.6432, -1.71198

Charges guide

Per unit incl. 2 persons and electricity	€ 17,70 - € 33,20
extra person	€ 3,10 - € 6,30
child (2-17 yrs)	€ 3,10 - € 6,00

FRANCE – Sanchey

Kawan Village Lac de Bouzey

19 rue du Lac, F-88390 Sanchey (Vosges)
t: 03 29 82 49 41   e: lacdebouzey@orange.fr
alanrogers.com/FR88040   www.lacdebouzey.com

Accommodation: ☑Pitch ☑Mobile home/chalet ☐Hotel/B&B ☐Apartment

Open all year, Camping Lac de Bouzey is 8 km. west of Épinal, at the start of the Vosges Massif. The 147 reasonably level grass pitches are separated by very tall trees and some hedging giving varying amounts of shade. There are 107 for touring, all with electricity (6-10A) and 100 fully serviced. They are on a gently sloping hillside above the lake and there are views over the lake and its sandy beaches. In high season there is entertainment for all ages, especially teenagers, and the site will be very lively. Many watersports may be enjoyed, from pedaloes to canoes, windsurfing and sailing. The large, imposing building at the entrance to the site houses a restaurant and bar with terraces overlooking the lake, and the underground disco. Two bars by the lake suggest that the lakeside is popular with the public in summer but the camping area is quiet, separated by a road and well back and above the main entrance. It is well placed for exploring the hills, valleys, lakes and waterfalls of the south of Alsace Lorraine.

You might like to know

The entertainment team organise nightly shows and a Kids' Club. Accompanied walks in the surrounding forest take in the local flora and fauna. Bicycle hire is available and there are many superb drives in the area, including la Route des Crètes, la Route des Vins and la Vallée des Lacs.

- ☑ Riding
- ☑ Pony trekking
- ☑ Archery
- ☑ Sailing
- ☑ Paintball
- ☑ Rock climbing
- ☑ Aerial walkways
- ☑ Go-karting
- ☑ 10-pin bowling
- ☑ Fishing

- ☑ Tennis/short tennis
- ☑ Canoeing/pedaloes
- ☑ Road/offroad cycling
- ☑ Rafting/canyoning

Facilities: The refurbished toilet block includes a baby room and one for disabled visitors (there are some gradients). Small, heated section in the main building with toilet, washbasin and shower is used in winter. Laundry facilities. Motorcaravan service point. Shop and bar (all year), restaurant and takeaway (1/3-1/11). Heated pool (1/5-30/9). Fishing. Riding. Games room. Archery. Bicycle hire. Internet access. Soundproofed room for cinema shows/discos (high season). Lake beach, bathing and boating. WiFi. Off site: Golf 8 km.

Open: All year.

Directions: Site is 8 km. west of Épinal on the D460. From Épinal follow signs for Lac de Bouzey and Sanchey. At western end of Sanchey turn south, site signed. GPS: 48.16692, 6.35990

Charges guide

Per unit incl. 2 persons and electricity	€ 23,00 - € 34,00
extra person	€ 6,00 - € 10,00
child (4-10 yrs)	free - € 7,00
dog	free - € 4,00

Stowford Farm Meadows

Berry Down, Combe Martin, Ilfracombe EX34 0PW (Devon)
t: 01271 882476 e: enquiries@stowford.co.uk
alanrogers.com/UK0690 www.stowford.co.uk

Accommodation: ☑Pitch ☑Mobile home/chalet ☐ Hotel/B&B ☐ Apartment

Stowford Farm is a friendly, family park set in 500 acres of the rolling North Devon countryside, available for recreation and walking, yet within easy reach of five local beaches. The touring park and its facilities have been developed in the fields and farm buildings surrounding the attractive old farmhouse and provide a village like centre with a comfortable spacious feel. There are 710 pitches on five slightly sloping meadows separated by Devon hedges of beech and ash. The numbered and marked pitches, some with hardstanding, are accessed by hard roads, most have electricity (10/16A) and there are well placed water points. Stowford also provides plenty to keep the whole family occupied without leaving the park, including woodland walks and horse riding from the park's own stables. The Old Stable Bar offers entertainment in high season including barn dances, discos, karaoke and other musical evenings.

You might like to know

This site is set in 500 acres of rolling Devon countryside, with mature woodland and lush green (caravan and camping) meadows lined with beech and ash hedges.

- ☑ Riding
- ☑ Pony trekking
- ☑ Cycling (road)
- ☑ Sports field
- ☑ Sailing
- ☑ Golf
- ☑ Hiking
- ☑ Fishing
- ☑ Woodland walks

Facilities: Five toilet blocks, each looked after by resident wardens, are fully equipped and provide good facilities. Laundry facilities and dishwashing. The newest block has underfloor heating and facilities for disabled visitors. Superior facilities for disabled visitors and private family washrooms are beside reception. Well stocked shop (with holiday goods and gas). Good value takeaway with restaurant area. Bars and entertainment in season. Indoor pool (22x10 m; heated Easter-Oct) at a small charge. Riding. 18-hole pitch and putt. Crazy golf. 'Kiddies kar' track (all charged). Games room. Large play area. Games and activities organised in high season. WiFi. ATM. Woodland walks. Max. 2 dogs (separate areas). Off site: Fishing and boat launching 4 miles.

Open: All year.

Directions: From Barnstaple take A39 towards Lynton. After 1 mile turn left on B3230. Turn right at garage on A3123 and park is 1.5 miles on the right. GPS: 51.174983, -4.05475

Charges guide

Per unit incl. 2 persons	
and electricity	£ 10,40 - £ 23,00
extra person	free - £ 4,50
child (5-12 yrs)	free - £ 4,50
dog	£ 1,60 - £ 2,60

UNITED KINGDOM – Upper Sheringham

Woodlands Caravan Park

Holt Road, Upper Sheringham NR26 8TU (Norfolk)
t: 01263 823802   e: enquiries@woodlandscaravanpark.co.uk
alanrogers.com/UK3435   www.woodlandscaravanpark.co.uk

Accommodation: ☑Pitch ☑Mobile home/chalet ☐ Hotel/B&B ☐ Apartment

This pleasant caravan park is set in parkland in the beautiful surroundings of north Norfolk's protected heathland, next to Sheringham Park (National Trust). There are 225 sloping grass pitches with 216 having electricity (10A). They are in two main areas for caravans and motorcaravans (tents are not accepted). A major feature of this site is the superb new toilet block with electronically controlled showers. There are many lovely local walks including one to the beach (1.5 miles). The park is within easy reach of Holt, Cromer and Sheringham, with the major bird watching areas of Blakeney, Cley and Salthouse also within 30 minutes drive. There is a good bar on site with entertainment at weekends and the excellent Pinewood Park Leisure Club is adjacent to the park. The Club has swimming pools, sauna, spa, gym and other fitness facilities at a discounted rate for those staying at Woodlands.

You might like to know
The nearby Hilltop Outdoor Centre offers a range of family activities including action-packed Adventure Days.

☑ Riding
☑ Cycling (road)
☑ Crafts
☑ Sailing
☑ Golf
☑ Hiking
☑ Fishing
☑ Sauna
☑ Gym

Facilities: One excellent new toilet block provides all the necessary facilities including those for disabled visitors, baby changing and laundry. Well stocked shop. Gas supplies. Lounge bar and family bar with musical entertainment most weekends. Barbecues. Play area (2 acres, fenced and gated). Pinewood Park Leisure Club with indoor pool, gym, sauna. etc (all year). Off site: Bicycle hire and fishing 1.5 miles. Norfolk coast, golf and riding 2 miles. Sailing 7 miles. Scenic railway. Stately homes.

Open: 20 March - 31 October.

Directions: From Cromer take the A148 towards Holt, pass signs for Sheringham Park and site is on right (camping sign) just before Bodham village. GPS: 52.92093, 1.17445

Charges guide

Per unit incl. electricity	£ 17,00 - £ 25,00
awning	£ 3,50

Rivendale Caravan & Leisure Park

Buxton Road, Alsop-en-le-Dale, Ashbourne DE6 1QU (Derbyshire)
t: 01335 310311 e: enquiries@rivendalecaravanpark.co.uk
alanrogers.com/UK3850 www.rivendalecaravanpark.co.uk

Accommodation: ☑ Pitch ☑ Mobile home/chalet ☑ Hotel/B&B ☐ Apartment

This unusual park has been developed in the bowl of a hill quarry which was last worked over 50 years ago. The steep quarry walls shelter three sides with marvellous views over the Peak National Park countryside to the south. Near the entrance to the park is a renovated stone building which houses reception, shop, bar and a café/restaurant. Nearby are 136 level and landscaped pitches, mostly of a generous size with 16A electricity and a mix of hardstanding and grass. In two separate fields and a copse there is provision for 50 tents and that area includes a fishing lake. All the touring pitches are within easy reach of the central stone-built toilet block which is in keeping with the environment and provided with underfloor heating. A new lodge-type heated toilet block is at the entrance to the tent fields. For rent on the park are B&B rooms, camping pods, lodges and yurts. The park takes up about 11 acres and a further 26 acres belong to the owners, with certain parts suitable for walking.

Special offers
Free walking map when you book more than two nights in a pod, yurt, lodge or B&B.

You might like to know
We have now opened our own fishing lake on site. The nearby river Dove, Carsington and Tittesworth reservoirs are famous for trout fishing.

- ☑ Pony trekking
- ☑ Cycling (mountain biking)
- ☑ Sailing
- ☑ Golf
- ☑ Rock climbing
- ☑ Hiking
- ☑ Canoeing
- ☑ Climbing wall
- ☑ Fishing
- ☑ Birdwatching
- ☑ Windsurfing
- ☑ Hot-air ballooning
- ☑ Photography courses
- ☑ Tennis

Facilities: Good toilet facilities include some washbasins in cubicles for ladies, and an excellent en-suite room for disabled visitors. Laundry room. Shop (all essentials). Bar (evenings) and café with home-made and local food (open mornings, lunch and evenings, both with limited opening in low season). Packed lunches from reception. Special events monthly and games in main season. Hot tubs for hire, delivered to your pitch. Electric bicycles for hire. WiFi in some areas (charged). B&B, camping pods, lodges and yurts available. Off site: Riding 5 miles. Boat launching and sailing 8 miles. Golf 10 miles. Alton Towers 35 minutes drive.

Open: All year excl. 9 January - 2 February.

Directions: Park is 7 miles north of Ashbourne on the A515 to Buxton, on the eastern side of the road. It is well signed between the turnings east to Alsop Moor and Matlock (A5012), but take care as this is a very fast section of the A515. GPS: 53.106383, -1.760567

Charges guide

Per unit incl. 2 persons and electricity	£ 18,50 - £ 23,00
extra person	£ 2,50
child (4-15 yrs)	£ 2,00
dog	£ 2,00

Croft Farm Water & Leisure Park

Bredon's Hardwick, Tewkesbury GL20 7EE (Gloucestershire)
t: **01684 772321**   e: **enquiries@croftfarmleisure.co.uk**
alanrogers.com/UK4150   **www.croftfarmleisure.co.uk**

Accommodation: ☑ Pitch   ☑ Mobile home/chalet   ☐ Hotel/B&B   ☐ Apartment

Croft Farm is an AALA licensed Watersports Centre with Royal Yachting Association approved tuition available for windsurfing, sailing, kayaking and canoeing. The lakeside campsite has around 96 level pitches, with electric hook-ups (10A), but there are many seasonal units, leaving around 36 pitches for touring, plus some tent pitches. There are 36 gravel hardstandings with very little shade or shelter. Gym and Tonic is a fully equipped gymnasium with qualified instructors, sunbed and sauna. Sports massage, aromatherapy and beauty treatments are available by appointment. Activity holidays for families and groups are organised. Campers can use their own non-powered boats on the lake with reduced launching fees and there is river fishing. There are plans to include a launch ramp onto the river. Climb Bredon Hill (2 miles) for a panoramic view of the Severn and Avon Valleys. Places of interest include Bredon Barn, pottery and church, and the historic town of Tewkesbury with its Abbey, theatre and indoor swimming pool.

You might like to know

Accommodation is available in camping pods, with catering from the lakeside café and bar. The watersports school has wide experience in tuition for individuals, families and groups on the lake and nearby River Avon. Sailing boats, windsurfers and canoes are available to hire.

☑ Riding
☑ Archery
☑ Sailing
☑ Windsurfing
☑ Rafting
☑ Canoeing
☑ Kayaking
☑ Pedaloes
☑ Fitness/gym
☑ Fishing

Facilities: A recently modernised building has excellent facilities with spacious hot showers, plus some dishwashing sinks. A heated unit in the main building is always open and best for cooler months; this provides further WCs, washbasins and showers, laundry and facilities for disabled visitors. Gas. Cafe/bar (Fri-Sun low season, daily at other times). Takeaway. Gym. Playground. River fishing. Barrier and toilet block key (£5 deposit). Fenced dog exercise area. WiFi in the clubhouse (free to visitors spending £5 or over). Off site: Pub opposite. Tewkesbury 1.5 miles. Golf 3 miles. Riding 8 miles.

Open: 1 March - 14 November.

Directions: Bredon's Hardwick is midway between Tewkesbury and Bredon on B4080. Site entrance opposite Cross Keys Inn. From M5 exit 9 take A438 (Tewkesbury), at first lights turn right into Shannon Way. Turn right at next lights, into Northway Lane, cross motorway bridge. Turn left into housing estate and cross second bridge. At T-junction turn right on B4080, site is on left. GPS: 52.015967, -2.130267

Charges guide

Per unit incl. 2 persons, electricity and awning	£ 16,00
extra person (over 3 yrs)	£ 4,00
dog	£ 1,00

Tummel Valley Holiday Park

Tummel Bridge, Pitlochry PH16 5SA (Perth and Kinross)
t: 01882 634221   e: enquiries@parkdeanholidays.co.uk
alanrogers.com/UK7305 www.parkdeanholidays.co.uk

Accommodation: ☑ Pitch ☑ Mobile home/chalet ☐ Hotel/B&B ☐ Apartment

Set in the Tay Forest Park on the banks of the River Tummel, this large family holiday park is part of the Parkdean Group. Divided into two areas by the roadway, the main emphasis is on chalets to let on the side that overlooks the river. Privately owned caravan holiday homes and touring pitches are on the other, quieter side. The 26 touring pitches, open plan with hardstanding, electricity hook-up and a shared water point, overlook a small fishing lake, which is an added attraction for all the family. On arrival, you should turn right and park, then cross back to book in. The leisure complex with indoor and outdoor activities is on the river side, as is the reception office.

You might like to know
There is a regular bus service close to the site entrance for those wishing to explore the Perthshire Highlands.

- ☑ Riding
- ☑ Cycling *(road)*
- ☑ Sports field
- ☑ Outdoor pool
- ☑ Golf
- ☑ Fishing
- ☑ Nature trails
- ☑ Sauna
- ☑ Adventure play area

Facilities: The very clean toilet block (recently refurbished) has vanity style washbasins, preset showers and a bathroom in each section. Good facilities for disabled visitors. Well equipped laundry. Chemical disposal but no motorcaravan service point. Shop. Riverside entertainment complex with bar and terrace, restaurant and takeaway. Indoor heated pool and toddlers' splash pool. Solarium and sauna. Amusements. Separate area with pool tables. All weather sports court. Adventure play area. Crazy golf. Nature trails. Bicycle hire. Fishing. Note: all venues are non-smoking. Max. 2 dogs per unit. Off site: Golf and riding 10 miles. Buses leave near park entrance.

Open: Late March/Easter - 31 October.

Directions: Travel through Pitlochry. After 2 miles turn left on B8019 to Tummel Bridge (10 miles). Park is on both the left and right. Tourers should turn right and park, then return to reception on the left. GPS: 56.70742, -4.02002

Charges guide

Per unit incl. 4 persons and electricity	£ 13,00 - £ 32,00
dog	£ 2,00 - £ 3,00

Forest Holidays Glenmore

Aviemore PH22 1QU (Highland)
t: **01479 861271** e: **info@forestholidays.co.uk**
alanrogers.com/UK7680 www.forestholidays.co.uk

Accommodation: ☑Pitch ☑Mobile home/chalet ☐ Hotel/B&B ☐ Apartment

Forest Holidays is a partnership between the Forestry Commission and The Camping and Caravanning Club. This site is attractively laid out in a fairly informal style in several adjoining areas connected by narrow, part gravel, part tarmac roads, with access to the lochside. One of these areas, the Pinewood Area, is very popular and has 32 hardstandings (some distance from the toilet block). Of the 220 marked pitches on fairly level, firm grass, 122 have electricity (16A). This site with something for everyone would be great for family holidays. The Glenmore Forest Park lies close to the sandy shore of Loch Morlich amidst conifer woods and surrounded on three sides by the impressive Cairngorm mountains. There is regular snowfall in the winter months. The park is conveniently situated for a range of activities, including skiing (extensive lift system), orienteering, hill and mountain walking (way-marked walks), fishing and non-motorised watersports on the Loch.

You might like to know

Why not join in one of the Forest Survival weekends and learn some of the skills you would need to survive alone in the woods? Great fun for all the family!

☑ **Cycling** (mountain biking)
☑ **Archery**
☑ **Golf**
☑ **Rock climbing**
☑ **Skiing** (downhill)
☑ **Canoeing**
☑ **Fishing**
☑ **Orienteering**
☑ **Den building**
☑ **Abseiling**

Facilities: New toilet and shower blocks. Next to the site is a range of amenities including a well stocked shop (open all year), a café serving a variety of meals and snacks, and a Forestry Commission visitor centre and souvenir shop. Barbecues are not permitted in dry weather. Bicycle hire. Fishing. Sandy beach (Blue Flag). Off site: The Aviemore centre with a wide range of indoor and outdoor recreation activities including skiing 7 miles. Golf within 15 miles. Fishing and boat trips.

Open: All year.

Directions: Immediately south of Aviemore on B9152 (not A9 bypass) take B970 then follow sign for Cairngorm and Loch Morlich. Site entrance is on right past the loch. If travelling in winter, prepare for snow.
GPS: 57.167033, -3.694717

Charges guide

Per unit incl. 2 persons and electricity	£ 18,00 - £ 25,50
extra person	£ 5,00 - £ 8,50
child	£ 2,75 - £ 4,50

Glen Nevis Touring Park

Glen Nevis, Fort William PH33 6SX (Highland)
t: **01397 702191**   e: **camping@glen-nevis.co.uk**
alanrogers.com/UK7830   www.glen-nevis.co.uk

Accommodation: ☑ Pitch ☑ Mobile home/chalet   ☐ Hotel/B&B   ☐ Apartment

Just outside Fort William, in a most attractive and quiet situation with views of Ben Nevis, this spacious park is used by those on active pursuits as well as sightseeing tourists. It comprises eight quite spacious fields, divided between caravans, motorcaravans and tents (steel pegs required). It is licensed for 250 touring caravans but with no specific tent limits. The large touring pitches, many with hardstanding, are marked with wooden fence dividers, 174 with electricity (13A) and 100 also have water and drainage. The park becomes full in the peak months but there are vacancies each day. If reception is closed (possible in low season) you site yourself. There are regular security patrols at night in busy periods. The park's own modern restaurant and bar with good value bar meals is a short stroll from the park, open to all. A well managed park with bustling, but pleasing ambience, watched over by Ben Nevis. Around 1,000 acres of the Glen Nevis estate are open to campers to see the wildlife and explore the area.

You might like to know

Fort William is the outdoor activity capital of the UK, home to Britain's highest mountain and some of the finest scenery that Europe has to offer.

☑ Cycling *(mountain biking)*   ☑ Skiing
☑ Diving   ☑ Snowboarding
☑ Golf   ☑ Ice Climbing
☑ Canyoning
☑ Rock climbing
☑ Hiking
☑ Kayaking
☑ 10-pin bowling
☑ Fishing
☑ Sailing

Facilities: The four modern toilet blocks with showers (extra showers in two blocks); and units for visitors with disabilities. An excellent block in Nevis Park (one of the eight camping fields) has some washbasins in cubicles, showers, further facilities for disabled visitors, a second large laundry room and dishwashing sinks. Motorcaravan service point. Shop (Easter-mid Oct), barbecue area and snack bar (May-mid Sept). Play area on bark. Off site: Pony trekking, golf and fishing nearby.

Open: 15 March - 31 October.

Directions: Turn off A82 to east at roundabout just north of Fort William following camp sign. GPS: 56.804517, -5.073917

Charges guide

Per person	£ 1,80 - £ 3,00
child (5-15 yrs)	£ 1,00 - £ 1,60
pitch incl. awning	£ 8,30 - £ 11,40
serviced pitch plus	£ 3,50 - £ 4,00

Ballinacourty House Touring Park

Glen of Aherlow, Tipperary (Co. Tipperary)
t: 062 565 59 e: info@camping.ie
alanrogers.com/IR9370 www.camping.ie

Accommodation: ☑ Pitch ☑ Mobile home/chalet   ☑ Hotel/B&B ☐ Apartment

Ballinacourty House and its cobble-stoned courtyard form the centrepiece of this south-facing park with views of the Galtee Mountains. Accessed by a tree-lined lane, the reception area is in part of the renovated 18th-century building, as is the adjoining restaurant. The park is level with 26 touring pitches with 6A electricity and 19 grassy pitches for tents. Some areas are shaded and there are open spaces to accommodate rallies and larger groups. Self-catering cottages and B&B are also available. This tranquil site is very appealing to families with young children. It is an excellent base from which to tour the Rock of Cashel, the Mitchelstown Caves, Swiss Cottage and the towns of Tipperary, Cahir and Cashel. The management has recently begun to keep farm animals in an enclosed part of the park and intends to enhance the estate's entire old walled garden. Activities in the area include horse riding and trekking, fishing for perch and brown trout, cycling, forest walks, three 18-hole golf courses and a leisure centre.

Facilities: Sanitary facilities provide free hot water and showers. Baby room. Laundry with ironing facilities. Campers' kitchen. Ice pack freezing. Licensed restaurant (early booking advised). Motorcaravan services. Gas supplies. Frisbee golf. TV and games rooms. Picnic benches. Tennis. Play area. Off site: Riding, fishing, golf within 5 miles.

Open: Easter - last Sunday in September.

Directions: Follow the N24 from Tipperary or Cahir to Bansha. Turn on to R663 for about 7 miles, passing Glen Hotel after 6 miles. Follow signs for Ballinacourty House.
GPS: 52.41614, -8.21047

Charges guide

Per unit incl. 2 persons and electricity	€ 24,00 - € 27,00
extra person	€ 5,00
child	€ 4,00

You might like to know

There are many superb walking trails in the area, ideal for families, and with plenty of information panels on the flora and fauna of the area, and picnic tables along the way. This corner of Ireland is also a haven for painters and photographers alike.

☑ Riding
☑ Pony trekking
☑ Tennis
☑ Cycling (mountain biking)
☑ Sports field
☑ Outdoor pool
☑ Golf
☑ Hiking
☑ Go-karting
☑ Fishing

Fossa Caravan & Camping Park

Fossa, Killarney (Co. Kerry)
t: 064 663 1497 e: fossaholidays@eircom.net
alanrogers.com/IR9590 www.fossacampingkillarney.com

Accommodation: ☑Pitch ☑Mobile home/chalet ☐ Hotel/B&B ☐ Apartment

This park is in the village of Fossa, ten minutes by car or bus (six per day) from Killarney town centre. Fossa Caravan Park has a distinctive reception building and hostel accommodation, a stimulating play area and shop. The park is divided in two – the touring caravan area lies to the right, tucked behind the main building and to the left is an open grass area mainly for campers. Touring pitches, with electricity (10/15A) and drainage, have hardstanding and are angled between shrubs and trees in a garden setting. To the rear at a higher level and discreetly placed are 30 caravan holiday homes, sheltered by the thick foliage of the wooded slopes which climb high behind the park. Not only is Fossa convenient for Killarney (5.5 km), it is also en-route for the famed Ring of Kerry, and makes an ideal base for walkers and golfers. Less than eight kilometers away are the famous walk up the Gap of Dunloe, and Carrantuohill, the highest mountain in Ireland.

You might like to know

The Dingle Peninsula offers fantastic views and winding lanes through small villages down to Slea Head, where you can see the Blasket Islands.

☑ Riding
☑ Pony trekking
☑ Tennis
☑ Cycling (road)
☑ Cycling (mountain biking)
☑ Outdoor pool
☑ Golf
☑ Hiking
☑ Fishing
☑ Mountaineering

Facilities: Modern toilet facilities include showers on payment. En-suite unit for campers with disabilities. Laundry room. Campers' kitchen. Shop. Takeaway (8/7-25/8). TV lounge. Tennis. Play area. Picnic area. Games room. Security patrol. Off site: Fishing and golf 2 km. Riding 3 km. Bicycle hire 5 km. Woodland walk into Killarney. A visit to Killarney National Park is highly recommended.

Open: 1 April - 30 September.

Directions: Approaching Killarney from all directions, follow signs for N72 Ring of Kerry/Killorglin. At last roundabout join R562/N72. Continue for 5.5 km. and Fossa is the second park to the right.
GPS: 52.07071, -9.58573

Charges guide

Per unit incl. 2 persons and electricity	€ 22,00 - € 26,00
extra person	€ 6,00
child (under 16 yrs)	€ 2,50
hiker/cyclist incl. tent	€ 8,00 - € 9,00

Mannix Point Touring Park

Cahirciveen (Co. Kerry)
t: 066 947 2806 e: mortimer@campinginkerry.com
alanrogers.com/IR9610 www.campinginkerry.com

Accommodation: ☑ Pitch ☑ Mobile home/chalet ☐ Hotel/B&B ☐ Apartment

A tranquil, beautifully located seashore park, it is no exaggeration to describe Mannix Point as a nature lovers' paradise. Situated in one of the most spectacular parts of the Ring of Kerry, overlooking the bay and Valentia Island, the rustic seven-acre park commands splendid views in all directions. The park road meanders through the level site and offers 42 pitches of various sizes and shapes, many with shelter and seclusion. There are 42 electrical connections (10A) available. A charming, old flower-bedecked fisherman's cottage has been converted to provide facilities including reception, an excellent campers' kitchen and a cosy sitting room with turf fire. There is no television, but compensation comes in the form of a knowledgeable, hospitable owner who is a Bord Fáilte registered local tour guide. A keen gardener, Mortimer Moriarty laid out the site over 20 years ago and his intention to cause as little disruption to nature as possible has succeeded. The site opens directly onto marshland which teems with wildlife.

Special offers
For the latest special offers, please visit the website: www.campinginkerry.com.

You might like to know
Sailing, surfing, windsurfing and water skiing are popular. The Atlantic Sailing Club (dinghies) operates from Mannix Point and member rates are available to campers. Fishing, fitness facilities, cycling and mountain biking are also possible.

☑ Riding
☑ Pony trekking
☑ Crafts
☑ Diving
☑ Rock climbing
☑ Hiking
☑ Canoeing
☑ Kayaking
☑ Pedaloes
☑ Birdwatching

☑ Whale watching trips
☑ Skellig tours
☑ Cruises
☑ Foreshore walks

Facilities: Toilet and shower facilities were clean when we visited. Modern and well equipped campers' kitchen and dining area. Comfortable campers' sitting room. Laundry facilities with washing machines and dryer. Motorcaravan service point. Picnic and barbecue facilities. Fishing and boat launching from site.
Off site: Bicycle hire 800 m. Riding 3 km. Golf 14 km. Pubs, restaurants and shops 15 minutes walk. Watersports, bird watching, walking and photography. Local cruises to Skelligs Rock with free transport to and from the port for walkers and cyclists.

Open: 15 March - 15 October.

Directions: Park is 300 m. off the N70 Ring of Kerry road, 800 m. southwest of Cahirciveen (or Cahersiveen) on the road towards Waterville. GPS: 51.941517, -10.24465

Charges guide

Per unit incl. 2 persons and electricity	€ 27,00
extra person	€ 6,00

No credit cards.

BELGIUM – Jabbeke

Recreatiepark Klein Strand

Varsenareweg 29, B-8490 Jabbeke (West Flanders)
t: **050 811 440** e: **info@kleinstrand.be**
alanrogers.com/BE0555 www.kleinstrand.be

Accommodation: ☑ Pitch ☑ Mobile home/chalet ☐ Hotel/B&B ☐ Apartment

In a convenient location just off the A10 motorway and close to Bruges, this site is in two distinct areas divided by an access road. The touring section has 137 large pitches on flat grass separated by well-trimmed hedges; all have electricity and access to water and drainage. Though surrounded by mobile homes and seasonal caravans, this is a surprisingly relaxing area and the ambience should have been further enhanced in 2011 when a small park was created at its centre. Some children's leisure facilities are provided here, and there is a spacious bar and a snack bar with takeaway. The main site with all the privately-owned mobile homes is closer to the lake and this area has most of the amenities. These include the main reception building, restaurants, bar, shop and sports facilities. This is a family holiday site and offers a comprehensive programme of activities and entertainment in July and August. The lake is used for waterskiing and has a supervised swimming area with waterslides (high season).

You might like to know

There is a sports school where you can learn to waterski.

- ☑ Riding
- ☑ Tennis
- ☑ Cycling *(road)*
- ☑ Outdoor pool
- ☑ Waterskiing
- ☑ Golf
- ☑ Paintball
- ☑ Beach volleyball
- ☑ Watersports
- ☑ Teambuilding

Facilities: A single modern, heated, toilet block in the touring area provides good sized showers (charged) and vanity style open washbasins. Baby room. Basic facilities for disabled campers. Laundry. Dishwashing outside. Additional toilet facilities with washbasins in cubicles are behind the touring field reception building (July/Aug). Motorcaravan service point. Bar and snack bar. Children's playground. Fun pool for small children. In main park: restaurants, bar and snack bar, takeaways (all year). Shop (Easter-end Aug). Tennis courts and sports field. Waterski school; waterski shows (Sundays in July/Aug), Cycle hire. Cable TV point (incl.) and WiFi (charged, first hour free) on all pitches. Off site: Riding 5 km. Beach 8 km. Golf and sailing 10 km.

Open: All year.

Directions: Jabbeke is 12 km. southwest of Bruges. From A18/A10 motorways, take exit 6/6B signed Jabbeke. At roundabout take first exit signed for site. In 650 m on left-hand bend, turn left to site in 600 m.
GPS: 51.18448, 3.10445

Charges guide

Per unit incl. 6 persons and electricity	€ 17,00 - € 34,00
dog	€ 2,00

BELGIUM – Lichtaart

Camping Floréal Kempen

Herentalsesteenweg 64, B-2460 Lichtaart (Antwerp)
t: 014 556 120   e: kempen@florealclub.be
alanrogers.com/BE0665   www.florealclub.be

Accommodation: ☑Pitch ☑Mobile home/chalet ☐ Hotel/B&B ☐ Apartment

This is an attractive woodland site and is a member of the Floréal group. It is located close to the well known Purperen Heide, a superb nature reserve with 15 scenic footpaths leading through it. There are 207 pitches, of which only 26 are reserved for touring units. These are of a good size (100 sq.m. or more), all with 10A electricity and most with their own water supply. Several simple cabins are available for hikers, as well as fully equipped mobile homes. There are some good leisure facilities, including tennis and a multisports pitch, as well as a popular bar and restaurant. Day trips to Antwerp are very much a possibility. The old city is a gem with a great deal of interest, including over a thousand noted monuments, a diamond museum and the Rubens trail. Another popular visit is to the charming Bobbejaanland amusement park. There are miles of forest trails and the site's friendly managers will be pleased to recommend routes.

You might like to know
During your holiday, why not visit Bobbejaanland amusement park? It is just a few kilometres from the campsite.

- ☑ Riding
- ☑ Tennis
- ☑ Cycling (road)
- ☑ Sports field
- ☑ Outdoor pool
- ☑ Golf
- ☑ Aerial walkways
- ☑ Multisports court
- ☑ Football
- ☑ Basketball

Facilities: Toilet facilities are in need of some investment. When we visited cleaning and maintenance needed attention. Motorcaravan services. Shop. Bar. Restaurant. Tennis. Play area. Multisport terrain. Tourist information. Mobile homes for rent. Off site: Walking and cycling tracks. Golf. Antwerp. Bobbejaanlaand amusement park

Open: All year.

Directions: Approaching from Antwerp, head east on A21 motorway as far as exit 24 (Turnhout). Leave here and head south on N19 to Kasterlee, and then west on N123 to Lichtaart. Follow signs to the site.
GPS: 51.21024, 4.90423

Charges guide

Per unit incl. 2 persons	€ 11,00 - € 16,50
extra person	€ 3,25
child (3-11 yrs)	€ 2,50
dog (max. 1)	€ 3,00

NETHERLANDS – Wolphaartsdijk

Camping De Veerhoeve

Veerweg 48, NL-4471 NC Wolphaartsdijk (Zeeland)
t: **0113 581 155** e: **info@deveerhoeve.nl**
alanrogers.com/NL5580 **www.deveerhoeve.nl**

Accommodation: ☑ Pitch ☑ Mobile home/chalet ☐ Hotel/B&B ☐ Apartment

This is a family run site near the shores of the Veerse Meer, which is ideal for family holidays. It is situated in a popular area for watersports and is well suited for sailing, windsurfing and fishing enthusiasts, with boat launching 100 m. away. A sandy beach and recreation area ideal for children is only a five minute walk. As with most sites in this area there are many mature static and seasonal pitches. However, part of the friendly, relaxed site is reserved for touring units with 90 marked pitches on grassy ground, all with electrical connections. A member of the Holland Tulip Parcs Group.

You might like to know

Adults and children alike will love a trip on the historic steam railway, other interesting outings include Miniature Walcheren, the Delta Expo and the fish auction at Colijnsplaat.

- ☑ Riding
- ☑ Tennis
- ☑ Cycling *(road)*
- ☑ Sailing
- ☑ Surfing
- ☑ Windsurfing
- ☑ Golf
- ☑ Hiking
- ☑ Canoeing
- ☑ Diving
- ☑ Fishing

Facilities: Sanitary facilities in three blocks have been well modernised with full tiling. Hot showers are on payment. Laundry facilities. Motorcaravan services. Supermarket (all season). Restaurant and snack bar. TV room. Tennis. Playground and playing field. Games room. Bicycle hire. Fishing. Accommodation for groups. Max. 1 dog. WiFi (charged). Off site: Slipway for launching boats 100 m. Riding 2 km. Golf 5 km.

Open: 1 April - 30 October.

Directions: From N256 Goes - Zierikzee road take Wolphaartsdijk exit. Follow through village and signs to site (be aware - one of the site signs is obscured by other road signs and could be missed). GPS: 51.54678, 3.81345

Charges guide

Per unit incl. up to 4 persons and electricity	€ 20,00 - € 27,00
dog	€ 4,00

NETHERLANDS – Uitdam

Camping Jachthaven Uitdam

Zeedijk 2, NL-1154 PP Uitdam (Noord-Holland)
t: **0204 031 433** e: **info@campinguitdam.nl**
alanrogers.com/NL5720 **www.campinguitdam.nl**

Accommodation: ☑ **Pitch** ☑ **Mobile home/chalet** ☐ Hotel/B&B ☐ Apartment

Situated beside the Markermeer, which is used extensively for watersports, this large site has its own private yachting marina (300 yachts and boats). It has 200 seasonal and permanent pitches, many used by watersports enthusiasts, but also offers 260 marked tourist pitches (180 with 4/6A electricity) on open, grassy ground overlooking the water and 24 mobile homes to rent. There is a special area for campers with bicycles. Very much dominated by the marina, this site will appeal to watersports enthusiasts, with opportunities for sailing, windsurfing and swimming, or for fishing, but it is also on a pretty stretch of coast. Much construction was underway when we visited, but this was mainly in the seasonal areas. All the touring pitches have been upgraded with new drainage and there are new cabins for rent. Uitdam is 15 km. northeast of Amsterdam and is close to the ancient, small towns of Marken, Volendam and Monnickendam, which are well worth a visit.

You might like to know
Camping Jachthaven Uitdam can be found on the edge of the protected Waterland nature area, the perfect environment for cycling, boating or just hiking.

- ☑ **Tennis**
- ☑ **Cycling** *(road)*
- ☑ **Sports field**
- ☑ **Sailing**
- ☑ **Windsurfing**
- ☑ **Golf**
- ☑ **Hiking**
- ☑ **Canoeing**
- ☑ **Fishing**
- ☑ **Children's pool**

Facilities: Two good toilet blocks and one rather basic one with toilets only. Good facilities include hot showers on payment, toilets, washbasins and a baby room. Motorcaravan services. Gas supplies. Shop (1/4-1/10). Bar/restaurant (weekends and high season). TV room. Tennis. Playground and paddling pool. Bicycle hire. Fishing. Yacht marina (with fuel) and slipway. Watersports. Entertainment in high season. Off site: Riding 4 km. Sailing 6 km. Golf 12 km.

Open: 1 March - 1 November.

Directions: From A10, take exit S116 onto the N247 towards Volendam. Then take Monnickendam exit south in direction of Marken on N518, then Uitdam. Site is just outside Uitdam. GPS: 52.42780, 5.07347

Charges guide

Per unit incl. 2 persons	€ 22,50
tent incl. 2 persons	€ 15,50 - € 19,00
extra person (over 3 yrs)	€ 3,00
boat on trailer	€ 7,00

Camping Lauwersoog

Strandweg 5, NL-9976 VS Lauwersoog (Groningen)
t: **0519 349 133** e: **info@lauwersoog.nl**
alanrogers.com/NL6090 www.lauwersoog.nl

Accommodation: ☑Pitch ☑Mobile home/chalet ☐ Hotel/B&B ☐ Apartment

The focus at Camping Lauwersoog is very much on the sea and watersports. One can have sailing lessons or hire canoes and, with a new extension, there is direct access to the beach from the site. There are 550 numbered pitches with 300 for tourers. Electricity (10A) is available at 275 large pitches and 125 have water, drainage, electricity and cable connections. The pitches are on level, grassy fields (some beside the beach), partly separated by hedges and some with shade from trees. A new building in the marina houses a restaurant, bar, shop and laundry, and also provides beautiful views over the Lauwersmeer. The site's restaurant specialises in seafood and even the entertainment programmes for all ages have a water theme. Youngsters can play on the beach or in a new covered play area, whilst adults may join sailing trips organised from the site, or walk and cycle through the Lauwersmeergebied (a national park) or perhaps, if the tide is low, even walk to Schiemonnikoog.

You might like to know
We also offer cruises, bike rides and walks with a guide. Summer night outings looking for deer.

- ☑ **Riding**
- ☑ **Cycling** *(road)*
- ☑ **Sailing**
- ☑ **Windsurfing**
- ☑ **Diving**
- ☑ **Canoeing**
- ☑ **Kayaking**
- ☑ **Go-karting**
- ☑ **Fishing**

Facilities: The two toilet blocks for tourers provide washbasins, preset showers and child size toilets. Facilities for disabled visitors. Laundry. Campers' kitchen. Ice service. Motorcaravan service. Shop. Restaurant (all year), bar and snack bar including takeaway service (1/4-1/10). New play area with bouncy castle. Minigolf at the beach. Sailing school. Canoe hire. Surfing lessons (July/Aug). Horse riding as well as bicycle and go-kart hire on site. Boules. WiFi. Extensive entertainment programme for all ages in high season. Torch useful. Off site: Golf 8 km.

Open: All year.

Directions: Follow N361 from Groningen north to Lauwersoog and then follow site signs. GPS: 53.40205, 6.21732

Charges guide

Per unit incl. 2 persons and 10A electricity	€ 28,50 - € 31,50
extra person	€ 4,75
dog	€ 4,75

Recreatiecentrum De Adelhof

Vledderweg 19, NL-8381 AB Vledder (Drenthe)
t: 0521 381 440   e: info@adelhof.nl
alanrogers.com/NL6125   www.adelhof.nl

Accommodation: ☑Pitch ☑Mobile home/chalet   ☐ Hotel/B&B   ☐ Apartment

With a fine location close to the large nature reserves of the Drents Friese Wold and Het Land van Oost, Recreatiecentrum De Adelhof is an ideal base for a cycling holiday in Drenthe, with miles of cycle tracks in the area. This is also a good site for anglers with a well stocked fishing lake. De Adelhof has 140 spacious touring pitches spread over several fields. The pitches are surrounded by bushes and shrubs to ensure privacy. They are generally around 100 sq.m. and all have electricity. Several attractive children's play areas have been created in each of the fields. One field in particular is reserved for families with dogs. There is a lively activity programme in high season. Activities include craft work, treasure hunts, theatre and musical evenings. The café/restaurant is the focal point here and is also the location for musical evenings. Here you can also play billiards, darts or watch TV. There are also a number of chalets available for rent.

You might like to know

At Ascension and Whitsun and for six weeks in high season, a professional programme of recreational activities is arranged. There are several idyllic cycling and walking trails in the park, and fishing is available in the large central pond. The park also has a café/restaurant, snack bar, camping shop and several playgrounds.

- ☑ Riding
- ☑ Pony trekking
- ☑ Tennis
- ☑ Cycling (road)
- ☑ Sports field
- ☑ Outdoor pool
- ☑ Hiking
- ☑ 10-pin bowling
- ☑ Fishing
- ☑ Table tennis

- ☑ Minigolf
- ☑ Bicycle hire
- ☑ Go-kart rental

Facilities: Four toilet blocks with all the usual facilities (one open in winter, cleaning can be variable). Small shop (end April-end Aug). Café/restaurant and snack bar (April-Nov). Large fishing lake with carp. Children's farm. Play areas. All-weather tennis. Minigolf. Bicycle and go-kart hire. Football field. Internet access. WiFi in some areas (charged). Professional entertainment team (spring holidays and high season). Off site: Municipal outdoor swimming pool (end April-beginning Sept, charged). Cycle and walking trails. Miramar Museum. Speelstad Oranje adventure park. Dwingelerveld national park. Nearby towns of Steenwijk, Meppel, Assen and Heerenveen.

Open: All year.

Directions: Vledder is 10 km. northeast of Steenwijk. From A38 motorway take the Steenwijk exit and follow N855 north to Frederiksoord and Vledder. The site is just before the village to the right. GPS: 52.85178, 6.19845

Charges guide

Per unit incl. 2 persons and electricity	€ 23,00
extra person	€ 3,50

NETHERLANDS – Biddinghuizen

Molecaten Park Flevostrand

Strandweg 1, NL-8256 RZ Biddinghuizen (Flevoland)
t: **0320 288 480** e: **info@flevostrand.nl**
alanrogers.com/NL6212 www.molecaten.nl/flevostrand

Accommodation: ☑ Pitch ☑ Mobile home/chalet ☐ Hotel/B&B ☐ Apartment

Flevostrand is a family site with direct access to Lake Veluwe's sandy beach. All the pitches here are large and sunny, and you may have a choice between pitches on the inner dyke (where no cars are allowed) or pitches closer to the lake on the outer dyke area, where you can park your car on your pitch. The site has a large marina with a pier and slipway, from where boat launching is possible (boat hire is available). There are various play areas and heated indoor and outdoor pools. Flevostrand (Flevo beach) is located on land reclaimed from the sea and was developed in the late 1960s. Despite this recent history, trees have matured rapidly in the area, and there are some good walks in the adjacent Wolderwijd forest. Alternatively, and in stark contrast, the Six Flags theme park (formerly Walibi) is close, and a little further you will find the old fishing port of Harderwijk, dating back to 1230.

You might like to know

Flevostrand is the place to be for surfers and sailing enthusiasts. If you enjoy watersports, the sailing and surfing courses on offer will help you improve your technique.

☑ Tennis
☑ Cycling *(road)*
☑ Sports field
☑ Outdoor pool
☑ Archery
☑ Sailing
☑ Surfing
☑ Windsurfing
☑ Kitesurfing
☑ Waterskiing

☑ Paintball
☑ Hiking
☑ Canoeing
☑ Fishing

Facilities: Restaurant with bar and terrace, takeaway. Indoor pool and outdoor pool with children's pool (all heated). Tennis courts. Play areas. Beach volleyball. Bicycle and boat hire. Marina with slipway. Mobile homes and chalets to rent. Off site: Walking and cycling. Six Flags theme park. Harderwijk.

Open: 1 April - 1 November.

Directions: Take exit 26 from A28 motorway (to Harderwijk/Lelystad) and follow signs to Lelystad (N302). After you have crossed the bridge (4.5 km), take first right turn at the roundabout towards Kampen (Harderdijk). Follow this road to Kampen and turn right after 3 km. The site is well signposted. GPS: 52.385401, 5.629088

Charges guide

Per unit incl. 2 persons and electricity	€ 15,50 - € 30,00
extra person	€ 3,90
child (2-10 yrs)	€ 2,90
dog	€ 3,90

NETHERLANDS – Sevenum

Recreatiecentrum De Schatberg

Midden Peelweg 5, NL-5975 MZ Sevenum (Limburg)
t: 0774 677 777   e: info@schatberg.nl
alanrogers.com/NL6510   www.schatberg.nl

Accommodation: ☑Pitch ☑Mobile home/chalet   ☐ Hotel/B&B   ☐ Apartment

In a woodland setting of 96 hectares, this family run campsite is more reminiscent of a holiday village, with a superb range of activities that make it an ideal venue for families. Look out for the deer! A large site with 1,100 pitches and many mobile homes and seasonal or weekend visitors, there are 500 touring pitches. All have electricity (6/10/16A Europlug), cable, water and drainage and average 100-150 sq.m. in size. They are on rough grass terrain, mostly with shade, but not separated. Forty pitches have private sanitary facilities (two with sauna and jacuzzi). Road noise can be heard in some areas of this large campsite. The site is well situated for visits to Germany and Belgium, and easily accessible from the port of Zeebrugge. The surrounding countryside offers the opportunity to enjoy nature, either by cycling or walking. For the more 'stay on site' visitor, the location is excellent with several lakes for fishing, windsurfing and swimming, plus an extensive range of activities and a heated outdoor swimming pool.

You might like to know
By the site entrance is a natural pool with a sandy beach, a sunbathing area, a small port and several playgrounds. A little further on is the surfing and fishing lake.

- ☑ **Cycling** *(road)*
- ☑ **Sports field**
- ☑ **Outdoor pool**
- ☑ **Windsurfing**
- ☑ **Golf**
- ☑ **Aerial walkways**
- ☑ **10-pin bowling**
- ☑ **Fishing**
- ☑ **Trampoline**

Facilities: Five modern, fully equipped toilet blocks, supplemented by three small wooden toilet units to save night-time walks. Family shower rooms, baby baths and en-suite units for disabled visitors. Washing machines and dryers. Motorcaravan service point. Supermarket. Restaurant, bar and takeaway. Pizzeria. Pancake restaurant. Indoor and outdoor pools. Trampoline. Play areas. Fishing. Watersports. Bicycle hire. Games room. Bowling and an underground disco. Indoor Playground. Entertainment weekends and high season. New waterski track for 2012. WiFi (charged). Off site: Golf 0.5 km.

Open: All year.

Directions: Site is 15 km. west-northwest of Venlo. Leave the A67 Eindhoven - Venlo motorway at Helden, exit 38. Travel north on the 277 for 500 m. and site is signed at new roundabout. GPS: 51.382964, 5.976147

Charges guide

Per unit incl. 2 persons and electricity	€ 18,16 - € 44,56
incl. up to 4 persons and electricity	€ 22,70 - € 55,70

Kennemer Duincamping De Lakens

Zeeweg 60, NL-2051 EC Bloemendaal aan Zee (Noord-Holland)
t: **0235 411 570** e: **delakens@kennemerduincampings.nl**
alanrogers.com/NL6870 www.kennemerduincampings.nl

Accommodation: ☑ Pitch ☑ Mobile home/chalet ☐ Hotel/B&B ☐ Apartment

De Lakens is part of de Kennemer Duincampings group and is beautifully located in the dunes at Bloemendaal aan Zee. This site has 940 reasonably large, flat pitches with a hardstanding of shells. There are 410 for tourers (235 with 16A electricity) and the sunny pitches are separated by low hedging. This site is a true oasis of peace in a part of the Netherlands usually bustling with activity. From this site it is possible to walk straight through the dunes to the North Sea. Although there is no pool, there is the sea. A separate area is provided for groups and youngsters to maintain the quiet atmosphere. It is not far to Amsterdam or Alkmaar and its cheese market. We feel you could have an enjoyable holiday here.

You might like to know

Activities are organised for children and there is a playing area just for them on the beach, which features a pirate ship. There is a golf course 10 km. from the site.

- ☑ **Cycling** *(road)*
- ☑ **Crafts**
- ☑ **Surfing**
- ☑ **Hiking**
- ☑ **Swimming**
- ☑ **Basketball**
- ☑ **Volleyball**
- ☑ **Table tennis**
- ☑ **Kite flying**

Facilities: The six toilet blocks for tourers (two brand new) include controllable showers, washbasins (open style and in cabins), facilities for disabled visitors and a baby room. Launderette. Two motorcaravan service points. Bar/restaurant and snack bar. Supermarket. Adventure playgrounds. Bicycle hire. Entertainment programme in high season for all. Dogs are not accepted. Off site: Beach and riding 1 km. Golf 10 km.

Open: 20 March - 1 November.

Directions: From Amsterdam go west to Haarlem and follow the N200 from Haarlem towards Bloemendaal aan Zee. Site is on the N200, on the right hand side.
GPS: 52.40563, 4.58652

Charges guide

Per unit incl. 4 persons	€ 14,10 - € 27,45
incl. electricity	€ 18,40 - € 28,70
extra person	€ 4,20

Camping Wulfener Hals

Wulfener Hals Weg, D-23769 Wulfen auf Fehmarn (Schleswig-Holstein)
t: 043 718 6280 e: camping@wulfenerhals.de
alanrogers.com/DE3003 www.wulfenerhals.de

Accommodation: ☑ Pitch ☑ Mobile home/chalet ☐ Hotel/B&B ☐ Apartment

This a top class, all year round site suitable as a stopover or as a base for a longer stay. Attractively situated by the sea, it is a large, mature site (34 hectares) and is well maintained. It has over 800 individual pitches (half for touring) of up to 160 sq.m. in glades. Some are separated by bushes providing shade in the older parts, less so in the newer areas nearer the sea. There are many hardstandings and all pitches have electricity, water and drainage. A separate area has been developed for motorcaravans. It provides 60 extra large pitches, all with electricity, water and drainage, and some with TV aerial points, together with a new toilet block. There is lots to do for both young and old at Wulfener Hals, with a new heated outdoor pool and paddling pool (unsupervised), although the sea is naturally popular as well. The site also has many sporting facilities including its own golf courses and schools for watersports. A member of Leading Campings Group.

You might like to know
Swimming lessons for children are available on site.

☑ Riding
☑ Pony trekking
☑ Cycling (mountain biking)
☑ Outdoor pool
☑ Archery
☑ Sailing
☑ Surfing
☑ Windsurfing
☑ Kitesurfing
☑ Go-karting

☑ Diving
☑ Waterskiing
☑ Golf
☑ Canoeing
☑ Fitness/gym

Facilities: Five heated sanitary buildings have first class facilities including showers and both open washbasins and private cabins. Family bathrooms for rent. Facilities for children and disabled campers. Beauty, wellness and cosmetic facilities. Laundry. Motorcaravan services. Shop, bar, restaurants and takeaway (April-Oct). Swimming pool (May-Oct). Sauna. Solarium. Jacuzzi. Sailing, catamaran, windsurfing and diving schools. Boat slipway. Golf courses (18 holes, par 72 and 9 holes, par 27). Riding. Fishing. Archery. Well organised and varied entertainment programmes for children of all ages. Bicycle hire. Catamaran hire. Off site: Naturist beach 500 m. Village shop 2 km.

Open: All year.

Directions: From Hamburg take A1/E47 north direction Puttgarden, after crossing the bridge to Fehmarn first exit to the right to Avendorf. In Avendorf turn left and follow the signs for Wulfen and the site. GPS: 54.40805, 11.17374

Charges guide

Per unit incl. 2 persons and electricity	€ 14,60 - € 42,11
extra person	€ 4,10 - € 8,60
child (2-18 yrs)	€ 2,30 - € 7,40
dog	€ 1,00 - € 7,50

GERMANY – Wesel

Erholungszentrum Grav-Insel

Grav-Insel 1, D-46487 Wesel (North Rhine-Westphalia)
t: 028 197 2830 e: info@grav-insel.com
alanrogers.com/DE3202 www.grav-insel.de

Accommodation: ☑ Pitch ☑ Mobile home/chalet ☐ Hotel/B&B ☐ Apartment

Grav-Insel claims to be the largest family camping site in Germany, providing entertainment and activities to match, with over 2,000 permanent units. A section for 500 touring units runs beside the water to the left of the entrance and this area has been completely renewed. These pitches, all with 10A electricity, are flat, grassy, mostly without shade and of about 100 sq.m. A walk through the site takes you past a nature reserve and to the Rhine where you can watch the barges. Despite its size, this site is very well maintained, calm, clean and spacious and this is down to the family which started it 40 years ago. This site, on the border with Holland, is an excellent stop over for the north and east of Germany. However, once here, you may decide to stay longer to take advantage of the excellent restaurant (special evenings each week), bird watching on the private reserve or to visit Xanten with its Roman amphitheatre in the archaeological park.

You might like to know

Whether you are looking for relaxation, excitement, education or just some fun, the Duisburg-Nord Landscape Park has all you need.

☑ **Cycling** (road)
☑ **Sports field**
☑ **Outdoor pool**
☑ **Sailing**
☑ **Hiking**
☑ **Fishing**
☑ **Football**
☑ **Children's zoo**
☑ **Beach volleyball**
☑ **Motor boats**

Facilities: Excellent sanitary facilities, housed in a modern building below the bar/restaurant (open all year). Portacabin units in touring area to be renewed. Facilities for disabled visitors. Baby room. Launderette. Motorcaravan service point. Large supermarket. Entertainment area with satellite TV. WiFi. Solarium. Large play area. Boat park. Sailing. Fishing. Swimming. Football (coaching in high season). Entertainment in high season. Off site: Bus service 500 m. Nord Park Duisburg leisure complex 25 km. Kleve (Cleves) – birthplace of Anne of Cleves 30 km. Warner Bros Movie Park, Bottrop 30 km.

Open: All year.

Directions: Site is 5 km. northwest of Wesel. From the A3 take exit 6 and B58 towards Wesel, then right towards Rees. Turn left at sign for Flüren, through Flüren and left to site after 1.5 km. If approaching Wesel from the west (B58), cross the Rhine, turn left at first traffic lights and follow signs Grav-Insel and Flüren. GPS: 51.67062, 6.55600

Charges guide

Per unit incl. 2 persons and electricity	€ 10,00 - € 15,50
child (under 12 yrs)	€ 1,00 - € 1,50
dog	€ 0,50 - € 1,00

Camping & Ferienpark Teichmann

Zum Träumen 1A, D-34516 Vöhl-Herzhausen (Hessen)
t: 056 352 45 e: info@camping-teichmann.de
alanrogers.com/DE3280 www.camping-teichmann.de

Accommodation: ☑Pitch ☑Mobile home/chalet ☐ Hotel/B&B ☐ Apartment

Situated near the eastern end of the 27 km. long Edersee and the National Park Kellerwald-Edersee, this attractively set site is surrounded by wooded hills and encircles a six-hectare lake, which has separate areas for swimming, fishing and boating. Of the 460 pitches, 250 are for touring; all have 10A electricity and 50 have fresh and waste water connections. The pitches are on level grass, some having an area of hardstanding, and are separated by hedges and mature trees. At the opposite side of the lake from the entrance, there is a separate area for tents with its own sanitary block. The adjoining national park, a popular leisure attraction, offers a wealth of holiday/sporting activities including walking, cycling (there are two passenger ferries that take cycles), boat trips, cable car and much more. For winter sports lovers, the ski centre at Winterberg is only 30 km. away from this all year round site. This is an ideal family site, as well as being suited to country lovers who can enjoy the forest and lakeside walks/cycle tracks.

You might like to know

This site is open all year round and is just 30 km. from the winter sport centre at Winterberg.

☑ Riding
☑ Tennis
☑ Cycling (road)
☑ Golf
☑ Hiking
☑ Skiing (downhill)
☑ Canoeing
☑ Fishing
☑ Cable car

Facilities: Three good quality sanitary blocks can be heated and have free showers, washbasins (open and in cabins), baby rooms and facilities for wheelchair users. Laundry. Motorcaravan services. Café and shop (both summer only). Restaurant by entrance open all day (closed Feb). Watersports. Boat and bicycle hire. Lake swimming. Fishing. Minigolf. Tennis. Playground. Sauna. Solarium. Disco (high season). Internet access. Off site: New national park opposite site entrance. Riding 500 m. Golf 25 km. Cable car (bicycles accepted). Aquapark. Boat trips on the Edersee.

Open: All year.

Directions: Site is 45 km. from Kassel. From A44 Oberhausen - Kassel autobahn, take exit 64 for Diemelstadt and head south for Korbach. Site is between Korbach and Frankenberg on the B252 road, 1 km. to the south of Herzhausen at the pedestrian traffic lights.
GPS: 51.17550, 8.89067

Charges guide

Per unit incl. 2 persons and electricity	€ 25,00 - € 29,00

Gugel's Dreiländer Camping

Oberer Wald 3, D-79395 Neuenburg-am-Rhein (Baden-Württemberg)
t: 076 317 719 e: info@camping-gugel.de
alanrogers.com/DE3455 www.camping-gugel.de

Accommodation: ☑Pitch ☑Mobile home/chalet ☐ Hotel/B&B ☐ Apartment

Set in natural heath and woodland, Gugel's is an attractive site with 220 touring pitches, either in small clearings in the trees, in open areas or on a hardstanding section used for overnight stays. All have electricity (16A), and some also have water, waste water and satellite TV connections. Opposite is a meadow where late arrivals and early departures may spend the night. There may be some road noise near the entrance. The site may become very busy in high season and on Bank Holidays but you should always find room. The excellent pool and wellness complex add to the attraction of this all year site. There is a social room with satellite TV where guests are welcomed with a glass of wine and a slide presentation of the attractions of the area. The Rhine is within walking distance. Neuenburg is ideally placed for enjoying and exploring the south of the Black Forest, and for night stops when travelling from Frankfurt to Basel on the A5 autobahn. The permanent caravans, with their pretty gardens, are away from the touring area.

You might like to know

Basel, Freiburg, Colmar and Breisach are old towns with minsters and cathedrals. They have a rich cultural heritage, but also boast modern shopping quarters and can be enjoyed in an afternoon.

☑ Riding
☑ Tennis
☑ Cycling (road)
☑ Sports field
☑ Golf
☑ Fitness/gym
☑ Fishing
☑ Beach volleyball
☑ Nordic walking

Facilities: Three good quality, heated sanitary blocks include some washbasins in cabins. Baby room. Facilities for disabled visitors. Laundry facilities. Motorcaravan services. Shop. Excellent restaurant. Takeaway (weekends and daily in high season). Wellness centre. Indoor/outdoor pool. Boules. Tennis. Fishing. Minigolf. Barbecue. Beach bar. Bicycle hire. Community room with TV. Activity programme (high season). Play areas. Off site: Riding 1.5 km. Golf 5 km. Neuenburg, Breisach, Freiburg, Basel and the Black Forest.

Open: All year.

Directions: From autobahn A5 take Neuenburg exit, turn left, then almost immediately left at traffic lights, left at next junction and follow signs for 2 km. to site (called 'Neuenburg' on most signs). GPS: 47.79693, 7.55

Charges guide

Per unit incl. 2 persons and electricity	€ 22,00 - € 26,50
extra person	€ 6,50
child (2-15 yrs)	€ 3,00
dog	€ 3,00

GERMANY – Krün-Obb

Alpen-Caravanpark Tennsee

Am Tennsee 1, D-82494 Krün-Obb (Bavaria (S))
t: 088 251 70   e: info@camping-tennsee.de
alanrogers.com/DE3680 www.camping-tennsee.de

Accommodation: ☑Pitch ☑Mobile home/chalet ☐ Hotel/B&B ☐ Apartment

Tennsee is an excellent, friendly site in truly beautiful surroundings high up (1,000 m) in the Karwendel Alps with super mountain views, and close to many famous places of which Innsbruck (44 km) and Oberammergau (26 km) are two. Mountain walks are plentiful, with several lifts close by. It is an attractive site with good facilities including 164 serviced pitches with individual connections for electricity (up to 16A and two connections), gas, TV, radio, telephone, water and waste water. The other 80 pitches all have electricity and some of these are available for overnight guests at a reduced rate. Reception and comfortable restaurants, a bar, cellar youth room and a well stocked shop are all housed in attractive buildings. Many activities and excursions are organised to local attractions by the Zick family, who run the site in a very friendly, helpful and efficient manner.

You might like to know
The mountain station of the nearby cable car affords a wonderful view of the Isar Valley and the Alpine scenery beyond.

☑ Riding
☑ Tennis
☑ Archery
☑ Sailing
☑ Windsurfing
☑ Diving
☑ Golf
☑ Skiing *(downhill)*
☑ Fishing
☑ Paragliding

Facilities: The first class toilet block has underfloor heating, washbasins in cabins and private units with WC, shower, basin and bidet for rent. Unit for disabled guests with the latest facilities. Baby bath, dog bathroom and a heated room for ski equipment (with lockers). Washing machines, free dryers and irons. Gas supplies. Motorcaravan services. Cooking facilities. Shop. Restaurants (waiter, self service and takeaway). Bar. Solarium. Bicycle hire. Playground. WiFi (charged). Organised activities and excursions. Bus service to ski slopes in winter.
Off site: Fishing 400 m. Riding and golf 3 km.

Open: All year excl. 6 November - 15 December.

Directions: Site is just off main Garmisch-Partenkirchen - Innsbruck road no. 2 between Klais and Krün, 15 km. from Garmisch watch for small sign 'Tennsee & Barmsee' and turn right there for site. GPS: 47.49066, 11.25396

Charges guide

Per unit incl. 2 persons	€ 23,00 - € 26,00
extra person	€ 7,50 - € 8,00
child (6-16 yrs)	€ 3,00 - € 4,00
electricity per kWh	€ 0,70
dog	€ 3,30

Camping Havelberge am Woblitzsee

An den Havelbergen 1, Userin, D-17237 Gross Quassow (Mecklenburg-West Pomerania)
t: **039 812 4790** e: **info@haveltourist.de**
alanrogers.com/DE3820 www.haveltourist.de

Accommodation: ☑ Pitch ☑ Mobile home/chalet ☐ Hotel/B&B ☐ Apartment

The Müritz National Park is a very large area of lakes and marshes, popular for birdwatching as well as watersports, and Havelberge is a large, well equipped site to use as a base for enjoying the area. It is quite steep in places with many terraces, most with shade, less in newer areas, and views over the lake. There are 400 pitches in total with 330 good sized, numbered touring pitches (most with 16A Europlug electrical connections) and 230 pitches on a newly developed area to the rear of the site with water and drainage. Pitches on the new field are level and separated by low hedges and bushes but have no shade. Over 170 seasonal pitches with a number of attractive chalets and an equal number of mobile homes in a separate area. In the high season this is a busy park with lots going on to entertain family members of all ages, whilst in the low seasons this is a peaceful base for exploring an unspoilt area of nature. A member of Leading Campings Group.

You might like to know

Canoes (Canadian style or kayaks) and rowing boats are available for hire. For beginners, there are introductory canoeing courses.

- ☑ Riding
- ☑ Cycling *(road)*
- ☑ Sports field
- ☑ Crafts
- ☑ Archery
- ☑ Sailing
- ☑ Diving
- ☑ Waterskiing
- ☑ Hiking
- ☑ Aerial walkways

- ☑ Zip wires
- ☑ Canoeing
- ☑ Kayaking
- ☑ Fishing

Facilities: Four sanitary buildings (one new and of a very high standard) provide very good facilities, with private cabins, showers on payment and large section for children. Fully equipped kitchen and laundry. Motorcaravan service point. Small shop, modern restaurant, bar, takeaway and wellness (all 1/4-31/10). The lake provides fishing, swimming from a small beach and boats can be launched (over 5 hp requires a German boat licence). Canoes, rowing boats, windsurfers and bikes can be hired. Play areas and entertainment in high season. Internet access. Off site: Riding 1.5 km.

Open: All year.

Directions: From A19 Rostock - Berlin road take exit 18 and follow B198 to Wesenberg and go left to Klein Quassow and follow site signs. GPS: 53.30517, 13.00133

Charges guide

Per unit incl. 2 persons and electricity	€ 15,90 - € 31,50
extra person	€ 4,30 - € 6,80
child (2-14 yrs)	€ 1,60 - € 4,60
dog	€ 1,00 - € 4,60

CZECH REPUBLIC – Vrchlabi

Holiday Park Lisci Farma

Dolní Branna 350, CZ-54362 Dolní Branná (Vychodocesky)
t: **499 421 473** e: **info@liscifarma.cz**
alanrogers.com/CZ4590 www.liscifarma.cz

Accommodation: ☑Pitch ☑Mobile home/chalet ☐ Hotel/B&B ☐ Apartment

This is truly an excellent site that could be in Western Europe considering its amenities, pitches and welcome. However, Lisci Farma retains a pleasant Czech atmosphere. In the winter months, when local skiing is available, snow chains are essential. The 260 pitches are fairly flat, although the terrain is slightly sloping and some pitches are terraced. There is shade and some pitches have hardstanding. The site is well equipped for the whole family with its adventure playground offering trampolines for children, archery, beach volleyball, Russian bowling and an outdoor bowling court for older youngsters. A beautiful sandy, lakeside beach is 800 m. from the entrance. The more active amongst you can go paragliding or rock climbing, with experienced people to guide you. This site is very suitable for relaxing or exploring the culture of the area. Excursions to Prague are organised and, if all the sporting possibilities are not enough, the children can take part in the activities arranged by the entertainment team.

You might like to know
There is an excellent restaurant on site, specialising in traditional Bohemian cuisine.

- ☑ Riding
- ☑ Tennis
- ☑ Cycling (road)
- ☑ Cycling (mountain biking)
- ☑ Archery
- ☑ Sailing
- ☑ Rock climbing
- ☑ Hiking
- ☑ Fishing
- ☑ Paragliding

Facilities: Two good sanitary blocks, one near the entrance and another modern block next to the hotel, both include toilets, washbasins and spacious, controllable showers (on payment). Child size toilets and baby room. Toilet for disabled visitors. Sauna and massage. Launderette with sinks, hot water and a washing machine. Shop (15/6-15/9). Bar/snack bar with pool table. Games room. Swimming pool (6x12 m). Adventure style playground on grass with climbing wall. Trampolines. Tennis. Minigolf. Archery. Russian bowling. Paragliding. Rock climbing. Bicycle hire. Entertainment programme. Excursions to Prague. Off site: Fishing and beach 800 m. Riding 2 km. Golf 5 km.

Open: 1 May - 30 September.

Directions: Follow road no. 14 from Liberec to Vrchlabi. At the roundabout turn in the direction of Prague and site is about 1.5 km. on the right. GPS: 50.61036, 15.60264

Charges guide

Per unit incl. 2 persons, 2 children and electricity	CZK 400 - 920
extra person	CZK 90 - 120
child (5-12 yrs)	CZK 35 - 59
dog	CZK 39 - 59

Camping Frymburk

Frymburk 184, CZ-38279 Frymburk (Jihocesky)
t: **380 735 284** e: **info@campingfrymburk.cz**
alanrogers.com/CZ4720 www.campingfrymburk.cz

Accommodation: ☑Pitch ☑Mobile home/chalet ☐ Hotel/B&B ☐ Apartment

Camping Frymburk is beautifully located on the Lipno lake in southern Bohemia and is an ideal site. From this site, activities could include walking, cycling, swimming, sailing, canoeing or rowing and afterwards you could relax in the small, cosy bar/restaurant. You could enjoy a real Czech meal in one of the restaurants in Frymburk or on site. The site has 170 level pitches on terraces (all with 6A electricity, some with hardstanding and 4 have private sanitary units) and from the lower terraces on the edge of the lake there are lovely views over the water to the woods on the opposite side. A ferry crosses the lake from Frymburk where one can walk or cycle in the woods. The Dutch owner, Mr Wilzing, will welcome the whole family, personally siting your caravan. Children will be entertained by 'Kidstown' and the site has a small beach.

You might like to know

South Bohemia (Sumava) is the largest protected natural area in the Czech Republic, with an impressive mountain range over 120 km. long.

☑ **Cycling** (road)
☑ **Cycling** (mountain biking)
☑ **Crafts**
☑ **Windsurfing**
☑ **Rafting**
☑ **Hiking**
☑ **Canoeing**
☑ **Fishing**
☑ **Volleyball**

Facilities: Three immaculate toilet blocks with toilets, washbasins, preset showers on payment and an en-suite bathroom with toilet, basin and shower. Facilities for disabled visitors. Launderette. Restaurant and bar (10/5-15/9). Motorcaravan services. Playground. Canoe, bicycle, pedalos, rowing boat and surfboard hire. Kidstown. Volleyball competitions. Rafting. Bus trips to Prague. Torches useful. Internet access and WiFi. Off site: Shops and restaurants in the village 900 m. Golf 7 km. Riding 20 km.

Open: 29 April - 1 October.

Directions: Take exit 114 at Passau in Germany towards Freyung in Czech Republic. Continue on this road till Philipsreut and from there follow the no. 4 road towards Vimperk. Turn right a few kilometres after the border towards Volary on no. 141 road. From Volary follow no. 163 road to Horni Plana, Cerna and Frymburk. Site is on 163 road, after village. GPS: 48.655947, 14.170239

Charges guide

Per unit incl. 2 persons and electricity	CZK 460 - 810
extra person	CZK 80 - 130
child (under 12 yrs)	CZK 60 - 90
dog	CZK 50 - 60

No credit cards.

Camping Bucek

Tratice 170, CZ-27101 Nové Straseci (Stredocesky)
t: **313 564 212** e: **info@campingbucek.cz**
alanrogers.com/CZ4825 www.campingbucek.cz

Accommodation: ☑Pitch ☑Mobile home/chalet ☐ Hotel/B&B ☐ Apartment

Camping Bucek is a pleasant, Dutch owned site 40 km. west of Prague. Its proprietors also own Camping Frymburk (CZ4720). Bucek is located on the edge of woodland and has direct access to a small lake – canoes and rowing boats are available for hire, as well as sun loungers on the site's private beach. There are 100 pitches here, many with pleasant views over the lake, and all with electrical connections (6A). Shade is quite limited. Nearby, Revnicov is a pleasant small town with a range of shops and restaurants. The castles of Karlstejn and Krivoklát are also within easy reach, along with Karlovy Vary and Prague itself.

You might like to know

Prague, with its world class museums, galleries and cinemas is just 40 km. away.

- ☑ Riding
- ☑ Cycling *(road)*
- ☑ Cycling *(mountain biking)*
- ☑ Crafts
- ☑ Windsurfing
- ☑ Hiking
- ☑ Canoeing
- ☑ Fishing

Facilities: Renovated toilet blocks with free hot showers. Washing and drying machine. Direct lake access. Swimming pool. Pedaloes, canoes, lounger hire. Minigolf. Play area. Off site: Revnicov 2 km. with shops (including a supermarket), bars and restaurants. Karlovy Vary 10 km. Prague 40 km. Koniprusy caves.

Open: 24 April - 15 September.

Directions: From the west, take no. 6/E48 express road towards Prague. Site is close to this road, about 3 km. after the Revnicov exit and is clearly signed from this point. Coming from the east, ignore other camping signs and continue until Bucek is signed (to the north). GPS: 50.1728, 13.8348

Charges guide

Per unit incl. 2 persons and electricity	CZK 450 - 590
extra person	CZK 75 - 95
child (under 12 yrs)	CZK 50 - 60
dog	CZK 50 - 60

No credit cards.

CZECH REPUBLIC – Vernerovice

Camping Aktief

CZ-54982 Vernerovice (Kralovehradecky)
t: 491 582 138 e: bert.mien@tiscali.cz
alanrogers.com/CZ4555 www.aktief.cz

Accommodation: ☑ Pitch ☑ Mobile home/chalet ☑ Hotel/B&B ☐ Apartment

Camping Aktief is a small, rural site on the outskirts of the village of Vernerovice. The site is located close to the Polish border, east of the Krkonose (or Giant) Mountains. The spectacular rock formations of Adrspach and Teplice nad Metuji are close at hand. This is a small site with just 20 pitches (all with 6A electricity), located in a tranquil and protected area with many fruit trees. From the campsite there are fine views around the surrounding rolling meadows and hills. The friendly Dutch owners have developed Camping Aktief as an important hiking centre. Plenty of other activities are also organised here, and detailed walking and cycle routes are available (in Dutch). Bert and Mien van Kampen, the site owners, are happy to share their knowledge of the local area, including a number of good restaurants. They also organise special tours, including visits to a local brewery and glassworks. Bikes, mountain bikes and fishing equipment are available for hire on site. In peak season, a weekly barbecue is organised.

Facilities: Modern toilet block with underfloor heating. Sauna. Mobile home for rent (max 6 people). Accommodation in luxuriously converted farm buildings. Off site: Bus stop 200 m. Railway station 2 km. Hiking and cycle trails. Fishing.

Open: 15 April - 31 October.

Directions: Vernerovice is located in the northeast of the country, just 1 km from the Polish border. From route 302 between Broumov and Mieroszow (Poland) take the exit at Mezimisti and, in Vernerovice, follow signs to the campsite. GPS: 50.616409, 16.228651

Charges guide

Per unit incl. 2 persons and electricity € 14,50

You might like to know

We organise an annual three-day walk of 50/100 km. for the Juliana public holiday. During most of the year, customised walks through the remote countryside can be arranged. Snowshoes, bicycles, mountain bikes and fishing rods can be hired.

☑ Horse riding
☑ Pony trekking
☑ Tennis
☑ Cycling (road)
☑ Cycling (mountain biking)
☑ Sports field
☑ Outdoor pool
☑ Rock climbing
☑ Hiking
☑ Snow skiing

☑ Cross country skiing
☑ Snowboarding
☑ Climbing wall
☑ Microlight flights
☑ Go-karting

SLOVAKIA – Liptovsky Trnovec

Mara Camping

SK-03222 Liptovsky Trnovec (Zilina)
t: 044 559 8458   e: atc.trnovec@atctrnovec.sk
alanrogers.com/SK4915   www.maracamping.sk

Accommodation: ☑Pitch ☑Mobile home/chalet   ☐ Hotel/B&B   ☐ Apartment

This is a good Slovakian site beside the Liptovská Mara reservoir, also close to the Tatra Mountains which are popular for climbing, hiking and mountain biking. The lake can be used for sailing, surfing, boating and pedaloes and some of this equipment may be rented on the site. Bicycles are also available for hire. There are 250 pitches, all used for touring units and with 14A electricity. With tarmac access roads, the level pitches are on a circular, grassy field and as pitching is rather haphazard, the site can become crowded in high season. Mature trees provide some shade, but in general this is an open site. There are several bars with snack and takeaway services on site with a restaurant nearby (300 m). The site is close to the historic cities of Liptovsky Mikulás (6 km), Vlkolinec (on the UNESCO World Heritage list) and Pribylina.

You might like to know
This site is situated on the banks of the Liptovsky Mara dam, the largest in Slovakia. The reservoir is popular with lovers of water and outdoor sports. Liptovsky Mara enjoys ideal conditions for yachting and windsurfing, with opportunities for fishing, sightseeing trips and mountain biking.

☑ **Cycling** (mountain biking)
☑ **Sailing**
☑ **Windsurfing**
☑ **Golf**
☑ **Rafting**
☑ **Rock climbing**
☑ **Hiking**
☑ **Canoeing**
☑ **Kayaking**
☑ **Fishing**

Facilities: Two good modern toilet blocks have British style toilets, washbasins in cabins and showers. Facilities for disabled visitors. Washing machines. Campers' kitchen. Bar with covered terrace and takeaway service. Basic playground. Minigolf. Fishing. Bicycle hire. Canoe hire and boat rental. Games room with arcade machines. Beach. Off site: New Tatralandia Aqua Park nearby. Walking in the Lower Tatra Mountains, or serious climbing in the Higher Tatra Mountains.

Open: 30 April - 30 October.

Directions: From E50 road take exit for Liptovsky Mikulás and turn left towards Liptovsky Trnovec on 584 road. Continue alongside the lake to site on the left.
GPS: 49.111135, 19.545946

Charges guide

Per unit incl. 2 persons	
and electricity	€ 20,00
extra person	€ 10,00
child (3-15 yrs)	€ 3,00 - € 3,50
dog	€ 2,00

Fårup Sø Camping

Fårupvej 58, DK-7300 Jelling (Vejle)
t: **75 87 13 44** e: **faarup-soe@dk-camp.dk**
alanrogers.com/DK2048 www.dk-camp.dk/faarup-soe

Accommodation: ☑ Pitch ☑ Mobile home/chalet ☐ Hotel/B&B ☐ Apartment

This site was originally set up in the woodlands of Jelling Skov where local farmers each had their own plot. Owned since January 2004 by the Dutch/Danish Albring family, this is a rural location on the Fårup Lake. Many trees have been removed to give the site a welcoming, open feel. There are 250 grassy pitches, mostly on terraces (from top to bottom the height difference is 53 m). The 35 newest terraced pitches provide beautiful views of the countryside and the Fårup lake. There are 200 pitches for touring units, most with 10A electricity, and some tent pitches without electricity. A new heated swimming pool (min. 25°C), a whirlpool (free of charge) and an indoor play area for children have been added. Next to the top toilet block is a barbecue area with a terrace and good views. A neighbour rents out water bikes and takes high season excursions onto the lake with a real Viking Ship. During the last weekend of May, the site celebrates the Jelling Musical Festival when it is advisable to book in advance.

You might like to know

There is an excellent animal park just 8 km. from this site.

- ☑ Riding
- ☑ Pony trekking
- ☑ Cycling (road)
- ☑ Sports field
- ☑ Outdoor pool
- ☑ Golf
- ☑ Canoeing
- ☑ Pedaloes
- ☑ Fishing
- ☑ Boat launching

Facilities: One modern and one older toilet block have British style toilets, open style washbasins and controllable hot showers. Family shower rooms. Baby room. Facilities for disabled visitors. Laundry. Campers' kitchen. Motorcaravan services. Shop (bread to order). New heated swimming pool and whirlpool. Indoor play area. Playgrounds. Minigolf. Games room. Pony riding. Lake with fishing, watersports and Viking ship. Activities for children (high season). Internet. Off site: Golf and riding 2 km. Lion Park 8 km. Boat launching 10 km. Legoland 20 km.

Open: 1 April - 30 September.

Directions: From Vejle take the 28 road towards Billund. In Skibet turn right towards Fårup Sø, Jennum and Jelling and follow the signs to Fårup Sø. GPS: 55.73614, 9.41777

Charges guide

Per person	DKK 61
child (3-11 yrs)	DKK 35
pitch	DKK 15 - 35
electricity	DKK 28

Jesperhus Feriecenter & Camping

Legindvej 30, DK-7900 Nykobing Mors (Viborg)
t: 96 70 14 00 e: jesperhus@jesperhus.dk
alanrogers.com/DK2140 www.jesperhus.dk

Accommodation: ☑ Pitch ☑ Mobile home/chalet ☐ Hotel/B&B ☐ Apartment

Jesperhus is an extensive, well organised and busy site with many leisure activities, adjacent to Blomsterpark (flower park). It is a TopCamp site with 662 numbered pitches, mostly in rows with some terracing, divided by shrubs and trees and with shade in parts. Many pitches are taken by seasonal, tour operator or rental units, so advance booking is advised for peak periods. Electricity (6A) is available on all pitches and water points are in all areas. With all the activities at this site an entire holiday could be spent here regardless of the weather, although Jesperhus is also an excellent centre for touring. The indoor and outdoor pool complex (daily charge) has three pools, diving boards, water slides with the 'black hole', spa pools, saunas and a solarium. Although it may appear to be just part of Jutland, Mors is an island in its own right surrounded by the lovely Limfjord. It is joined to the mainland by a fine 2,000 m. bridge at the end of which are signs to Blomsterpark (Northern Europe's largest flower park) and the campsite.

You might like to know

The indoor facilities provide a wide range of sporting activities including squash and climbing.

☑ Riding
☑ Tennis
☑ Cycling (road)
☑ Cycling (mountain biking)
☑ Outdoor pool
☑ Golf
☑ Go-karting
☑ 10-pin bowling
☑ Fishing
☑ Beach volleyball

Facilities: Four good sanitary units are cleaned three times daily. Facilities include washbasins in cubicles or with divider/curtain, family and whirlpool bathrooms (on payment), suites for babies and disabled visitors. Free sauna. Superb kitchens and a fully equipped laundry. Supermarket (1/4-1/11). Restaurant. Bar. Café, takeaway. Pool complex with spa facilities. Bowling. Minigolf. Tennis. Go-karts and other outdoor sports. Children's 'playworld'. Playgrounds. Pets corner. Golf. Fishing pond. Practice golf (3 holes). Off site: Beach and riding 2 km. Bicycle hire 6 km.

Open: All year.

Directions: From south or north, take road 26 to Salling Sund bridge, site is signed Jesperhus, just north of the bridge. GPS: 56.75082, 8.81580

Charges guide

Per person	DKK 75
child (1-11 yrs)	DKK 55
pitch	free - DKK 50
electricity	DKK 40

DENMARK – Fjerritslev

Klim Strand Camping

Havvejen 167, Klim Strand, DK-9690 Fjerritslev (Nordjylland)
t: 98 22 53 40 e: ksc@klim-strand.dk
alanrogers.com/DK2170 www.klim-strand.dk

Accommodation: ☑ Pitch ☑ Mobile home/chalet ☐ Hotel/B&B ☐ Apartment

A large family holiday site right beside the sea, Klim Strand is a paradise for children. It is a privately owned TopCamp site with a full complement of quality facilities, including its own fire engine and trained staff. The site has 460 numbered touring pitches, all with electricity (10A), laid out in rows, many divided by trees and hedges and shade in parts. Some 220 of these are fully serviced with electricity, water, drainage and TV hook-up. On site activities include an outdoor water slide complex, an indoor pool, tennis courts and pony riding (all free). A wellness spa centre is a recent addition. For children there are numerous play areas, an adventure playground with aerial cable ride and a roller skating area. There is a kayak school and a large bouncy castle for toddlers. Live music and dancing are organised twice a week in high season. Suggested excursions include trips to offshore islands, visits to local potteries, a brewery museum and bird watching on the Bygholm Vejle. A member of Leading Campings Group.

You might like to know
The North Sea Oceanarium is the biggest aquarium in northern Europe.

- ☑ Riding
- ☑ Tennis
- ☑ Cycling *(road)*
- ☑ Outdoor pool
- ☑ Golf
- ☑ Kayaking
- ☑ Fitness/gym
- ☑ Fishing

Facilities: Two good, large, heated toilet blocks are central, with spacious showers and some washbasins in cubicles. Separate children's room. Baby rooms. Bathrooms for families (some charged) and disabled visitors. Two smaller units are by reception and beach. Laundry. Well equipped kitchens and barbecue areas. TV lounges. Motorcaravan services. Pizzeria. Supermarket, restaurant and bar (all season). Pool complex. Sauna, solariums, whirlpool bath, hairdressing rooms, fitness room. Wellness centre. Internet café. TV rental. Play areas. Crèche. Bicycle hire. Cabins to rent. Off site: Golf 10 km. Boat launching 25 km.

Open: 26 March - 24 October.

Directions: Turn off Thisted - Fjerritslev 11 road to Klim from where site is signed. GPS: 57.133333, 9.166667

Charges guide

Per unit incl. 2 persons and electricity	DKK 305 - 355
extra person	DKK 75
child (1-11 yrs)	DKK 55
dog	DKK 25

DENMARK – Grenå

Fornæs Camping

Stensmarkvej 36, DK-8500 Grenå (Århus)
t: 86 33 23 30 e: fornaes@1031.inord.dk
alanrogers.com/DK2070

Accommodation: ☑Pitch ☑Mobile home/chalet ☐ Hotel/B&B ☐ Apartment

In the grounds of a former farm, Fornæs Camping is about 5 km. from Grenå. From reception, a wide, gravel access road descends through a large grassy field to the sea. Pitches to the left are mostly level, to the right slightly sloping with some terracing and views of the Kattegat. The rows of pitches are divided into separate areas by colourful bushes and each row is marked by a concrete tub containing a young tree and colourful flowers. Fornæs has 320 pitches of which 240 are for tourers, the others being used for seasonal visitors. All touring pitches have 10A electricity. At the foot of the site is a pebble beach with a large grass area behind it for play and sunbathing. There is also an attractive outdoor pool near the entrance with two slides, a paddling pool, sauna, solarium and whirlpool. A comprehensive room serves as a restaurant, takeaway and bar, and there is a new games room. Fornæs provides a good base from which to explore this part of Denmark or for taking the ferry to Hjelm island or to Sweden.

You might like to know
There are a number of attractive, fully equipped wooden chalets on this site, all available for rent.

- ☑ Riding
- ☑ Outdoor pool
- ☑ Sailing
- ☑ Golf
- ☑ Fishing
- ☑ Minigolf
- ☑ Sauna
- ☑ Adventure playground

Facilities: Two toilet blocks have British style toilets, washbasins in cabins and controllable hot showers (on payment). Child-size toilets. Family shower rooms. Baby room. Facilities for disabled campers. Fully equipped laundry. Campers' kitchen. Motorcaravan service point. Shop. Café/grill with bar and takeaway (evenings). Swimming pool (80 sq.m) with paddling pool. Sauna and solarium. Play area and adventure playground. Games room with satellite TV. Minigolf. Fishing. Watersports. Off site: Golf and riding 5 km.

Open: 15 March - 20 September.

Directions: From Århus follow the 15 road towards Grenå and then the 16 road towards town centre. Turn north and follow signs for Fornæs and the site. GPS: 56.45602, 10.94107

Charges guide

Per person	DKK 67 - 75
child (1-12 yrs)	DKK 38 - 42
electricity (10A)	DKK 28

Credit cards 5% surcharge.

Odda Camping

Borsto, N-5750 Odda (Hordaland)
t: **41 32 16 10** e: **post@oppleve.no**
alanrogers.com/NO2320 www.oppleve.no

Accommodation: ☑ **Pitch** ☑ **Mobile home/chalet** ☐ Hotel/B&B ☐ Apartment

Bordered by the Folgefonna glacier to the west and the Hardangervidda plateau to the east and south, Odda is an industrial town with electro-chemical enterprises based on zinc mining and hydro-electric power. This site has been attractively developed on the town's southern outskirts. It is spread over 2.5 acres of flat, mature woodland, which is divided into small clearings by massive boulders. Access is by well tended tarmac roads which wind their way among the trees and boulders. There are 55 tourist pitches including 36 with electricity. The site fills up in the evenings and can be crowded with facilities stretched from the end of June to early August. The site is just over a kilometre from the centre of town, on the shores of the Sandvin lake (good salmon and trout fishing) and on the minor road leading up the Buar Valley to the Buar glacier, Vidfoss Falls and Folgefonna ice cap. It is possible to walk to the ice face but in the later stages this is quite hard going!

You might like to know

The campsite is open all year, offering a wide range of summer and winter activities and the chance to experience nature and the great outdoors. These include winter orienteering and tours to waterfalls and glaciers.

- ☑ **Riding**
- ☑ **Tennis**
- ☑ **Cycling** (mountain biking)
- ☑ **Archery**
- ☑ **Paintball**
- ☑ **Rafting**
- ☑ **Rock climbing**
- ☑ **Hiking**
- ☑ **Skiing** (downhill)
- ☑ **Snowboarding**

- ☑ **Canoeing**
- ☑ **Water rugby**
- ☑ **Glacier walks**
- ☑ **Fishing**
- ☑ **Swimming**

Facilities: A single timber building at the entrance houses the reception office and the simple, but clean, sanitary facilities which provide for each sex, two WCs, one hot shower (on payment) and three open washbasins. A new building provides additional unisex toilets, showers and laundry facilities. Small kitchen with dishwashing facilities. Mini shop. Off site: Town facilities close.

Open: All year.

Directions: Site is on the southern outskirts of Odda, signed off road to Buar, with a well marked access. GPS: 60.05320, 6.54380

Charges guide

Per person	NOK 10
tent and car	NOK 110
caravan or motorcaravan	NOK 130
electricity	NOK 40

No credit cards.

Lærdal Ferie & Fritidspark

Grandavegens, N-6886 Lærdal (Sogn og Fjordane)
t: **57 66 66 95** e: **info@laerdalferiepark.com**
alanrogers.com/NO2375 www.laerdalferiepark.com

Accommodation: ☑ Pitch ☑ Mobile home/chalet ☑ Hotel/B&B ☑ Apartment

This site is beside the famous Sognefjord, the longest fjord in the world. It is ideally situated if you want to explore the glaciers, fjords and waterfalls of the region. The 100 pitches are level with well trimmed grass and connected by tarmac roads and are suitable for tents, caravans and motorcaravans. There are 80 electrical hook-ups. The fully licensed restaurant serves traditional meals as well as snacks and pizzas. The pretty little village of Laerdal, only 400 m. away, is well worth a visit. A walk among the old, small wooden houses is a pleasant and interesting experience. You can hire boats on the site for short trips on the fjord. Guided hiking, cycling and fishing trips are also available. The site also provides cabins, flats and rooms to rent, plus a brand new motel, all very modern and extremely tastefully designed.

You might like to know

Laerdal Ferie & Fritidspark is situated right on the famous Sognefjord, the longest and the deepest fjord in the world. The Norwegian Wild Salmon Centre is just 400 m. from site.

- ☑ Riding
- ☑ Tennis
- ☑ Cycling *(road)*
- ☑ Cycling *(mountain biking)*
- ☑ Golf
- ☑ Hiking
- ☑ Canoeing
- ☑ Fishing
- ☑ Beach volleyball

Facilities: Two modern and well decorated sanitary blocks with washbasins (some in cubicles), showers on payment, and toilets. Facilities for disabled visitors. Children's room. Washing machine and dryer. Kitchen. Motorcaravan services. Small shop. Bar, restaurant and takeaway (20/5-5/9). TV room. Playground. Motorboats, rowing boats, canoes, bicycles and pedal cars for hire. Bicycle hire. Fishing. WiFi at reception. Off site: Cruises on the Sognefjord 400 m. The Norwegian Wild Salmon Centre 400 m. Riding 500 m. Golf 12 km. The Flåm railway 40 km.

Open: All year,
by telephone request 1 Nov - 14 March.

Directions: Site is on road 5 (from the Oslo - Bergen road, E 16) 400 m. north of Laerdal village centre. GPS: 61.10037, 7.46986

Charges guide

Per unit incl. 2 persons and electricity	NOK 210
extra person	NOK 50
child (4-15 yrs)	NOK 25

Kjørnes Camping

N-6856 Sogndal (Sogn og Fjordane)
t: **57 67 45 80** e: **camping@kjornes.no**
alanrogers.com/NO2390 www.kjornes.no

Accommodation: ☑Pitch ☑Mobile home/chalet ☐ Hotel/B&B ☑ Apartment

Kjørnes Camping is idyllically situated on the Sognefjord, 3 km. from the centre of Sogndal. It occupies a long open meadow which is terraced down to the waterside. The site has 100 pitches for camping units (all with electricity), nine cabins and two apartments for rent. Located at the very centre of the 'fjord kingdom' by the main no. 5 road, this site is the ideal base from which to explore the Sognefjord. You are within a short drive (maximum one hour) from all the major attractions including the Jostedal glacier, the Nærøyfjord, the Flåm Railway, the Urnes Stave Church and Sognefjellet. This site is ideal for those who enjoy peace and quiet, lovely scenery or a spot of fishing. Access is via a narrow lane with passing places, which drops down towards the fjord three kilometres from Sogndal.

You might like to know

The Sogn Folkemuseum is a fascinating museum with activities for all ages. Its exhibits include old homes, buildings and farm animals, and it explains how the local farmers worked the land in the 1800s.

- ☑ **Cycling** (road)
- ☑ **Cycling** (mountain biking)
- ☑ **Rafting**
- ☑ **Rock climbing**
- ☑ **Hiking**
- ☑ **Aerial walkways**
- ☑ **Fishing**
- ☑ **Glacier walks**
- ☑ **Swimming**

Facilities: A new, high quality sanitary building was added in 2008. Baby room. Facilities for disabled visitors. A new building provides a kitchen with cooking facilities, dishwasher, a dining area overlooking the fjord, and laundry facilities. Small shop (20/6-20/8). Satellite TV, WiFi and Internet. Off site: Hiking, glacier walks, climbing, rafting, walking around Sognefjord. Details from reception. Bicycle hire 3 km.

Open: 1 May - 1 October.

Directions: Site is off the Rv 5, 3 km. east of Sogndal, 8 km. west of Kaupanger. GPS: 61.21164, 7.12108

Charges guide

Per unit incl. 2 persons

and electricity	NOK 260
extra person	NOK 30
child (4-16 yrs)	NOK 10

Trollveggen Camping

Horgheimseidet, N-6300 Åndalsnes (Møre og Romsdal)
t: 71 22 37 00 e: post@trollveggen.no
alanrogers.com/NO2452 www.trollveggen.no

Accommodation: ☑ Pitch ☑ Mobile home/chalet ☐ Hotel/B&B ☐ Apartment

The location of this site provides a unique experience – it is set at the foot of the famous vertical cliff of Trollveggen (the Troll Wall), which is Europe's highest vertical mountain face. The site is pleasantly laid out in terraces with level grass pitches. The facility block, four cabins and the reception are all very attractively built with grass roofs. Beside the river is an attractive barbecue area where barbecue parties are sometimes arranged. This site is a must for people who love nature. The site is surrounded by the Troll Peaks and the Romsdalshorn Mountains with the rapid river of Rauma flowing by. Here in the beautiful valley of Romsdalen you have the ideal starting point for trips to many outstanding attractions such as 'The Troll Road' to Geiranger or to the Mandalsfossen waterfalls. In the mountains there are nature trails of various lengths and difficulties. The campsite owners are happy to help you with information. The town of Åndalsnes, 10 km. away, has a range of shops and restaurants.

You might like to know

The popular Atlanterhavsveien is a spectacular scenic road that winds its way along the coast between rocky outcrops and islands. It was voted 'Norwegian Construction of the Century'.

- ☑ Cycling *(mountain biking)*
- ☑ Outdoor pool
- ☑ Golf
- ☑ Rock climbing
- ☑ Hiking
- ☑ Canoeing
- ☑ Kayaking
- ☑ Fishing
- ☑ Glacier walking
- ☑ Paragliding
- ☑ Base jumping

Facilities: One heated toilet block provides washbasins, some in cubicles, and showers on payment. Family room with baby bath and changing mat, plus facilities for disabled visitors. Communal kitchen with cooking rings, small ovens, fridge and sinks (free hot water). Laundry facilities. Motorcaravan service point. Barbecue area (covered). Playground. Duck pond. WiFi throughout (free). Off site: Climbing, glacier walking and hiking. Fjord fishing. Sightseeing trips. The Troll Road. Mardalsfossen (waterfall). Geiranger and Åndalsnes.

Open: 10 May - 20 September.

Directions: Site is located on the E136 road, 10 km. south of Åndalsnes. It is signed. GPS: 62.49444, 7.758333

Charges guide

Per unit incl. 2 persons and electricity	NOK 229
extra person (over 4 yrs)	NOK 12

Neset Camping

N-4741 Byglandsfjord (Aust-Agder)
t: **37 93 42 55** e: **post@neset.no**
alanrogers.com/NO2610 www.neset.no

Accommodation: ☑Pitch ☑Mobile home/chalet ☐ Hotel/B&B ☐ Apartment

On a semi-promontory on the shores of the 40 km. long Byglandsfjord, Neset is a good centre for activities or as a stop en route north from the ferry port of Kristiansand (from England or Denmark). Neset is situated on well kept grassy meadows by the lake shore with the water on three sides and the road on the fourth, and provides 200 unmarked pitches with electricity and cable TV available. The main building houses reception, a small shop and a restaurant with fine views over the water. This is a well run, friendly site where one could spend an active few days. Byglandsfjord offers good fishing (mainly trout) and the area has marked trails for cycling, riding or walking in an area famous for its minerals.

You might like to know

The Setesdal valley is home to a number of museums devoted to minerals, silversmithing and other forms of art and handicraft.

- ☑ Riding
- ☑ Cycling (road)
- ☑ Cycling (mountain biking)
- ☑ Sailing
- ☑ Rafting
- ☑ Rock climbing
- ☑ Hiking
- ☑ Skiing (cross-country)
- ☑ Canoeing
- ☑ Fishing

Facilities: Three modern sanitary blocks which can be heated, all with comfortable hot showers (some on payment), washing up facilities (metered hot water) and a kitchen. Restaurant and takeaway (15/6-15/8). Shop (1/5-1/10). Campers' kitchen. Playground. Lake swimming, boating and fishing. Excellent new barbecue area and hot tub. Bicycle, canoe and pedalo hire. Climbing, rafting and canoeing courses arranged (including trips to see beavers and elk). Cross-country skiing possible in winter. Off site: Rock climbing wall. Marked forest trails.

Open: All year.

Directions: Site is on route 9, 2.5 km. north of the town of Byglandsfjord on the eastern shores of the lake. GPS: 58.68848, 7.80132

Charges guide

Per person	NOK 10
pitch	NOK 160
child (5-12 yrs)	NOK 5
electricity	NOK 30

Röstånga Camping & Bad

Blinkarpsvägen 3, S-260 24 Röstånga (Skåne Län)
t: 043 591 064   e: nystrand@msn.com
alanrogers.com/SW2630   www.rostangacamping.se

Accommodation: ☑Pitch ☑Mobile home/chalet ☐ Hotel/B&B ☐ Apartment

Beside the Söderåsen National Park, this scenic campsite has its own fishing lake and many activities for the whole family. There are 136 large, level, grassy pitches with electricity (10A) and a quiet area for tents with a view over the fishing lake. The tent area has its own service building and several barbecue places. A large holiday home and 14 pleasant cabins are available to rent all year round. A pool complex adjacent to the site provides a 50 m. swimming pool, three children's pools and a water slide, all heated during peak season. Activities are arranged on the site in high season, including a children's club with exciting activities such as treasure hunts and gold panning, and for adults aquarobics, Nordic walking and tennis. The Söderåsen National Park offers hiking and bicycle trails. The friendly staff will be happy to help you to plan interesting excursions in the area.

You might like to know

An activity leader organises a wide selection of activities and events, which are free of charge for all campers.

☑ Riding
☑ Pony trekking
☑ Tennis
☑ Cycling *(road)*
☑ Cycling *(mountain biking)*
☑ Outdoor pool
☑ Golf
☑ Hiking
☑ Canoeing
☑ Fishing

Facilities: Four good, heated sanitary blocks with free hot water and facilities for babies and disabled visitors. Laundry with washing machines and dryers. Kitchen with cooking rings, oven and microwave. Motorcaravan service point. Small shop at reception. Bar, restaurant and takeaway. Minigolf. Tennis. Fitness trail. Fishing. Canoe hire. Children's club. WiFi. Off site: Swimming pool complex adjacent to site (free for campers as is a visit to the Zoo). Many golf courses nearby. Motor racing track at Ring Knutstorp 8 km.

Open: 21 April - 2 October.

Directions: From Malmö: drive towards Lund and follow road no. 108 to Röstånga. From Stockholm: turn off at Østra Ljungby and take road no. 13 to Röstånga. In Röstånga drive through the village on road no. 108 and follow the signs. GPS: 55.996583, 13.28005

Charges guide

Per unit incl. 2 persons and electricity	€ 25,00 - € 33,00

Hafsten Swecamp Resort

Hafsten 120, S-451 96 Uddevalla (Västra Götalands Län)
t: 052 264 4117   e: info@hafsten.se
alanrogers.com/SW2725   www.hafsten.se

Accommodation: ☑ Pitch   ☑ Mobile home/chalet   ☐ Hotel/B&B   ☐ Apartment

This privately owned site on the west coast is situated on a peninsula overlooking the magnificent coastline of Bohuslän. Open all year, it is a lovely, peaceful, terraced site with a beautiful, shallow and child-friendly sandy beach and many nature trails in the vicinity. There are 190 touring pitches, all with electricity (10A), 100 with water and drainage. In all, there are 340 pitches including a tent area and 62 cabins of a high standard. There are plenty of activities available ranging from horse riding at the stables on the campsite's own farm to an 86 m. long water chute. Organised live music evenings with visiting performers are arranged during the summer. Almost any activity can be arranged on the site or elsewhere by the friendly owners if they are given advance notice. Amenities include two clean and well maintained service buildings, a pub, a fully licensed restaurant with wine from their own French vineyard, and a well stocked shop and a takeaway. Reception houses the new fitness and wellness facilities.

You might like to know

The site is located between Stromstad, known for its yachting harbour, and Gothenburg, Sweden's second largest city with two universities and the Liseberg amusement park.

- ☑ Riding
- ☑ Tennis
- ☑ Cycling (road)
- ☑ Cycling (mountain biking)
- ☑ Crafts
- ☑ Sailing
- ☑ Golf
- ☑ Hiking
- ☑ Canoeing
- ☑ Fishing

Facilities: Two heated sanitary buildings provide the usual facilities. Showers are on payment. Kitchen with good cooking facilities and dishwashing sinks. Dining room. Laundry facilities. Units for disabled visitors. Motorcaravan services. Shop. Restaurant, takeaway (1/6-31/8) and pub. Live music evenings. TV room. Relaxation centre with sauna and jacuzzi (charged). Well equipped gym. Water slide (charged). WiFi (charged). Riding. Minigolf. Tennis. Boules. Playground. Clay pigeon shooting. Boat hire (canoe, rowing, motor, pedalo). Outside gym/fitness area. Off site: Shopping centre and golf 13 km. Havets hus (marine museum) 30 km. Nordens Ark (animal park) 40 km.

Open: All year.

Directions: From the E6, north Uddevalla, at Torpmotet exit take the 161 road towards Lysekil. At the Rotviksbro roundabout take the 160 road towards Orust. The exit to the site is located further on road 2 km. on the left where four flags fly. Follow the signs for 4 km. along a one way road for motorcaravans and caravans.
GPS: 58.314683, 11.723333

Charges guide

Per pitch incl. electricity	SEK 230 - 355

Bredäng Camping Stockholm

Stora Sällskapets väg, S-127 31 Skärholmen (Stockholms Län)
t: 089 770 71   e: bredangcamping@telia.com
alanrogers.com/SW2842   www.bredangcamping.se

Accommodation: ☑ Pitch ☑ Mobile home/chalet   ☐ Hotel/B&B   ☐ Apartment

Bredäng is a busy city site, with easy access to Stockholm city centre. Large and fairly level, with very little shade, there are 380 pitches, including 115 with hardstanding and 204 with electricity (10A), and a separate area for tents. Reception is open from 08.00-23.00 in the main season (12/6-20/8), reduced hours in low season, and English is spoken. A Stockholm card is available, or a three-day public transport card from the Tube station. Stockholm has many events and activities, you can take a circular tour on a free sightseeing bus, various boat and bus tours, or view the city from the Kaknäs Tower (155 m). The nearest Tube station is five minutes walk; trains run about every ten minutes between 05.00 and 02.00, and the journey takes about twenty minutes. The local shopping centre is five minutes away and a two minute walk through the woods brings you to a very attractive lake and beach.

You might like to know

This site is within easy reach of Stockholm, but also very close to Lake Malaren and just 350 m. from the Mälarhöjdens open-air swimming area.

☑ Riding
☑ Tennis
☑ Cycling (road)
☑ Crafts
☑ Sailing
☑ Golf
☑ Hiking
☑ Canoeing
☑ Fishing

Facilities: Four heated sanitary units of a high standard provide British style WCs, controllable hot showers, with some washbasins in cubicles. One has a baby room, a unit for disabled visitors and a first aid room. Cooking and dishwashing facilities are in three units around the site. Laundry facilities. Motorcaravan services and car wash. Well stocked shop, bar, takeaway and fully licensed restaurant (all 1/5-31/8). Sauna. Playground. Off site: Fishing 500 m.

Open: 18 April - 9 October.

Directions: Site is about 10 km. southwest of city centre. Turn off E4/E20 at Bredängs signpost and follow clearly marked site signs.
GPS: 59.29560, 17.92315

Charges guide

Per unit incl. electricity	SEK 280 - 325
1 person tent	SEK 120 - 140

FINLAND – Ruovesi

Camping Haapasaaren Lomakylä

Haapasaarentie 5, FIN-34600 Ruovesi (Häme)
t: 044 080 0290   e: lomakyla@haapasaari.fi
alanrogers.com/FI2840   www.ruovedenhaapasaarenmatkailu.fi

Accommodation: ☑ Pitch   ☑ Mobile home/chalet   ☐ Hotel/B&B   ☐ Apartment

Haapasaaren is located on Lake Näsijärvi, around 70 km. north of Tampere in south western Finland. This is a well equipped site with a café and restaurant, a traditional Finnish outside dancing area and, of course, plenty of saunas! Rowing boats, canoes, cycles and, during the winter months, sleds are all available for rent. Fishing is very popular here. Pitches are grassy and of a good size. There is also a good range of accommodation to rent, including holiday cottages with saunas. The cosy restaurant, Jätkäinkämppä, has an attractive terrace and fine views across the lake. Alternatively, the site's café, Portinpieli, offers a range of snacks as well as Internet access. Haapasaaren's friendly owners organise a series of guided tours throughout the year. These include hiking and nature treks, berry and mushroom picking, and, during the winter, ice fishing and cross-country skiing. Helvetinjärvi National Park, one of the most dramatic areas of western Finland, is made up of deep gorges and dense forests.

You might like to know
Some great organised trips are on offer - why not try the berry- and mushroom-picking trips, some cross-country skiing or maybe even ice fishing and burbot catching?

- ☑ **Cycling** *(mountain biking)*
- ☑ **Sports field**
- ☑ **Skiing** *(downhill)*
- ☑ **Skiing** *(cross-country)*
- ☑ **Canoeing**
- ☑ **Fishing**
- ☑ **Rowing boats**
- ☑ **Nordic walking**
- ☑ **Sled**
- ☑ **Sauna**

Facilities: Café. Restaurant. Direct lake access. Saunas. Fishing. Minigolf. Boat and canoe hire. Bicycle hire. Guided tours. Play area. Tourist information. Chalets for rent. Off site: Walking and cycle routes. Boat trips. Helvetinjärvi National Park.

Open: All year.

Directions: From Helsinki, head north on the E12 motorway to Tampere and then northeast on N63-9 to Orivesi. Then, continue north on route 66 to Ruovesi and follow signs to the site. GPS: 61.99413, 24.069843

Charges guide

Per unit incl. 2 persons and electricity	€ 25,00
extra person	€ 4,00
child (under 15 yrs)	€ 2,00

FINLAND – Oulu

Nallikari Camping

Leiritie 10, FIN-90510 Oulu (Oulu)
t: 044 703 1353 e: nallikari.camping@ouka.fi
alanrogers.com/FI2970 www.nallikari.fi

Accommodation: ☑Pitch ☑Mobile home/chalet ☐ Hotel/B&B ☐ Apartment

This is probably one of the best sites in Scandinavia, set in a recreational wooded area alongside a sandy beach on the banks of the Baltic Sea, with the added bonus of the adjacent Eden Spa complex. Nallikari provides 200 pitches with electricity (175 also have water supply and drainage), plus an additional 78 cottages to rent, 28 of which are suitable for winter occupation. Oulu is a modern town, about 100 miles south of the Arctic Circle, that enjoys long, sunny and dry summer days. The Baltic however is frozen for many weeks in the winter and then the sun barely rises for two months. In early June the days are very long with the sun setting at about 23.30 and rising at 01.30! Nallikari, to the west of Oulu, is 3 km. along purpose-built cycle paths and the town has much to offer. Nordic walking, with or without roller blades, seems to be a recreational pastime for Finns of all ages! You might even be tempted to buy a pair of long, brightly coloured walking sticks yourself!

You might like to know

Great spa facilities can be found at this site – maybe you could try the Finnish custom of organising a meeting in the sauna facilities!

☑ Tennis

☑ Cycling (road)

☑ Golf

☑ Hiking

☑ Skiing (downhill)

☑ Aerial walkways

☑ Fishing

☑ Squash

☑ Beach volleyball

☑ Minigolf

Facilities: The modern shower/WC blocks also provide male and female saunas, kitchen and launderette facilities. Facilities for disabled visitors. Motorcaravan service point. Playground. Reception with café/restaurant (June-Aug), souvenir and grocery shop. TV room. WiFi. Bicycle hire. Off site: The adjacent Eden Centre provides excellent modern spa facilities where you can enjoy a day under the glass-roofed pool with its jacuzzis, saunas, Turkish baths and an Irish bath. Fishing 5 km. Golf 15 km.

Open: All year.

Directions: Leave road 4/E75 at junction with road 20 and head west down Kiertotie. Site well signed, Nallikari Eden, but continue on, just after traffic lights, cross a bridge and take the second on the right. Just before the Eden Centre turn right towards Leiritie and reception.
GPS: 65.02973, 25.41793

Charges guide

Per unit incl. 2 persons	€ 10,00 - € 18,00
extra person	€ 4,00
child (under 15 yrs)	€ 1,00
electricity	€ 4,50 - € 6,50

Been to any good campsites lately?
We have

You'll find them here...

... also here...

101 great campsites, ideal for your specific hobby,
pastime or passion

Want independent campsite reviews at your fingertips?

You'll find them here...

Over 3,000 in-depth campsite reviews at **www.alanrogers.com**

...and even here...

An exciting free app from iTunes, the Apple app store or the Android Market

Want to book your holiday on one of Europe's top campsites?

We can do it for you. No problem.

The best campsites in the most popular regions - we'll take care of everything

alan rogers ⬤ travel

alan rogers

Discover the best campsites in Europe
with Alan Rogers

alanrogers.com
01580 214000

index

AUSTRIA

West

Aktiv-Camping Prutz Tirol
Prutz 44

Camping Seehof
Kramsach 43

Ferienparadies Natterer See
Natters 42

BELGIUM

Flanders

Camping Floréal Kempen
Lichtaart 85

Recreatiepark Klein Strand
Jabbeke 84

CZECH REPUBLIC

Central Bohemia

Camping Bucek
Nové Straseci 101

East Bohemia

Camping Aktief
Vernerovice 102

North Bohemia

Holiday Park Lisci Farma
Vrchlabi 99

South Bohemia

Camping Frymburk
Frymburk 100

DENMARK

Jutland

Fårup Sø Camping
Jelling 104

Fornæs Camping
Grenå 107

Jesperhus Feriecenter & Camping
Nykobing Mors 105

Klim Strand Camping
Fjerritslev 106

FINLAND

Lapland

Nallikari Camping
Oulu 117

Southwest

Camping Haapasaaren Lomakylä
Ruovesi 116

FRANCE

Aquitaine

Airotel Camping de la Côte d'Argent
Hourtin-Plage 56

Camping le Tedey
Lacanau-Lac 57

Brittany

Castel Camping le Ty-Nadan
Locunolé 55

Côte d'Azur

Camping Green Park
Cagnes-sur-Mer 51

Languedoc-Roussillon

Camping la Sirène
Argelès-sur-Mer 63

Camping le Lamparo
Sainte Marie-en-Roussillon 62

Camping Village Homair La Palmeraie
Torreilles-Plage 61

Lorraine
Kawan Village Lac de Bouzey
Sanchey 73

Midi-Pyrénées
Camping l'Arize
La Bastide-de-Sérou 53

Camping le Montagnou
Le Trein d'Ustou 54

Camping Soleil du Pibeste
Agos-Vidalos 60

Pays de la Loire
Camping de l'Etang
Brissac 59

Provence
Camping des Princes d'Orange
Orpierre 50

Camping les Pêcheurs
Roquebrune-sur-Argens 70

Camping Résidence du Campeur
Saint Aygulf 69

Rhône Alpes
Campéole la Nublière
Doussard 68

Camping Caravaning l'Escale
Le Grand-Bornand 66

Camping le Parc Isertan
Pralognan-la-Vanoise 65

Camping les Dômes de Miage
Saint Gervais-les-Bains 67

Domaine le Pommier
Villeneuve-de-Berg 52

Flower Camping les Lanchettes
Peisey-Nancroix 64

Val de Loire
Leading Camping les Alicourts
Pierrefitte-sur-Sauldre 58

Vendée
Camping Domaine de la Forêt
Saint Julien-des-Landes 72

Castel Camping la Garangeoire
Saint Julien-des-Landes 71

GERMANY
North East
Camping Havelberge am Woblitzsee
Userin 98

North West
Camping Wulfener Hals
Wulfen 93

Erholungszentrum Grav-Insel
Wesel 94

South East
Alpen-Caravanpark Tennsee
Krün-Obb 97

index

South West

Camping & Ferienpark Teichmann
Vöhl   95

Gugel's Dreiländer Camping
Neuenburg   96

HUNGARY
Lake Balaton and District

Balatontourist Camping Füred
Balatonfüred   39

Balatontourist Camping Napfény
Révfülöp   41

The Great Plain

Martfü Health & Recreation Centre
Martfü   40

IRELAND
Shannon

Ballinacourty House Touring Park
Tipperary   81

South West

Fossa Caravan & Camping Park
Killarney   82

Mannix Point Camping & Caravan Park
Cahirciveen   83

ITALY
North East

Camping Arquin
Lana   26

Camping Corones
Rasen   27

Camping Lago di Levico
Levico Terme   32

Camping Punta Lago
Calceranica al Lago   31

Camping Residence Sägemühle
Prad am Stilfserjoch   30

Camping Seiser Alm
Völs am Schlern   29

Caravan Park Sexten
Sexten   28

Dolomiti Camping Village
Dimaro   25

North West

Camping Villaggio dei Fiori
San Remo   33

NETHERLANDS
Central

Molecaten Park Flevostrand
Biddinghuizen   90

North

Camping Lauwersoog
Lauwersoog   88

Recreatiecentrum De Adelhof
Vledder   89

South

Recreatiecentrum De Schatberg
Sevenum   91

West

Camping De Veerhoeve

Wolphaartsdijk   86

Camping Jachthaven Uitdam
Uitdam   87

Kennemer Duincamping De Lakens
Bloemendaal   92

NORWAY

South

Neset Camping
Byglandsfjord   112

Western Fjords

Kjørnes Camping
Sogndal   110

Lærdal Ferie & Fritidspark
Lærdal   109

Odda Camping
Odda   108

Trollveggen Camping
Åndalsnes   111

PORTUGAL

Alentejo

Zmar-Eco Camping Resort
Odemira   24

Lisbon & Vale do Tejo

Orbitur Camping Rio Alto
Póvoa de Varzim   23

SLOVAKIA

Centre

Mara Camping
Liptovsky Trnovec   103

SLOVENIA

Camping Bled
Bled   34

Camping Terme 3000
Moravske Toplice   35

Camping Terme Banovci
Verzej   38

Camping Terme Catez
Catez ob Savi   36

Camping Terme Ptuj
Ptuj   37

SPAIN

Andalucia

Camping Roche
Conil de la Frontera   21

Asturias

Camping Picos de Europa
Avin-Onis   22

Cataluña-Catalunya

Camping Internacional de Calonge
Calonge   20

index

Camping La Gaviota
Sant Pere Pescador 17

Camping Las Dunas
Sant Pere Pescador 19

Camping Las Palmeras
Sant Pere Pescador 18

SWEDEN
South
Bredäng Camping Stockholm
Skärholmen 115

Hafsten Swecamp Resort
Uddevalla 114

Röstånga Camping & Bad
Röstånga 113

SWITZERLAND
South
Camping Eienwäldli
Engelberg 49

Camping Grassi
Frutigen 45

Camping Jungfrau
Lauterbrunnen 48

Camping Lazy Rancho 4
Interlaken 47

Camping Manor Farm 1
Interlaken 46

UNITED KINGDOM
England
West Country
Stowford Farm Meadows
Ilfracombe 74

East of England
Woodlands Caravan Park
Sheringham 75

Heart of England
Rivendale Caravan & Leisure Park
Ashbourne 76

Croft Farm Water & Leisure Park
Tewkesbury 77

Scotland
Heart of Scotland
Tummel Valley Holiday Park
Pitlochry 78

Highlands and Islands
Forest Holidays Glenmore
Aviemore 79

Glen Nevis Caravan & Camping Park
Fort William 80